OVID

IN EXILE

Adrian Rădulescu

OVID

IN EXILE

VITA HISTRIA

VITA HISTRIA

Las Vegas ◊ Oxford ◊ Palm Beach

Published in the United States of America by
Histria Books, a division of Histria LLC
7181 N. Hualapai Way
Las Vegas, NV 89166 USA
HistriaBooks.com

Vita Histria is an imprint of Histria Books. Titles published
under the imprints of Histria Books are distributed
worldwide exclusively by the Casemate Group.

Library of Congress Control Number: 2018963976
ISBN 978-1-59211-020-9 (Softbound)
ISBN 978-1-59211-019-3 (Hardcover)

CONTENTS

PREFACE

I wrote the present volume to fill the need for a study on the life and work of Ovid in exile on the Black Sea coast, in Tomis, present-day Constanţa in Romania. I also wanted to place Ovid's life in exile in the context of the history of the Greek city-states on the coast and their relations with the native population, known as the Getae, one of the ancestors of the Romanian people. For Romanians, Ovid is a symbol of their participation in the creation of the lyrical values of human civilization.

This book was written in Constanta, ancient Tomis – so familiar to the author of these pages – within whose defensive walls, two thousand years ago, the magical lyre of the leading poet of cultivated society vibrated. Ovid had been banished from the imperial capital to spend the last years of his life in an undeserved exile, while fulfilling his destiny as a precursor of the Romanians whose history is marked by their Geto-Dacian and Latin origin and demonstrated by a vast array of archeological evidence, a linguistic treasury represented by many important Latin testimonies, all of which are amply illustrated in Trajan's Column, the Dadan Sarmizegetusa, and the triumphal monument of Adamclisi – Tropaeum Traiani.[1] Publius

---

[1]The triumphal monument Tropaeum Traiani, built by the Romans in the year A.D. 109, on the order of the Roman Emperor Trajan, commemorates a great

Ovidius Naso, the sensitive bard of love and suffering, son of Sulmo and citizen of Tomis, glorifies this heritage.

This volume is meant to enhance the reader's understanding of Ovid's poetry by following its natural evolution from Rome to Tomis. Had the poet not experienced the torment of exile we would not have today *The Letters from Pontus,* with their mature, sensitive expression, written in perfect verse inspired by genius.

Undoubtedly, the permanence of Ovid's work over the course of twenty centuries is explained both by his prodigious talent, as well as his exile in Tomis. These are the two existential conditions that have always attracted the curiosity of readers and the interest of researchers in chronicles and archives which disclose nothing more than the poet himself revealed after his banishment from Rome. As for Ovid's exile in Tomis, it seems to have been imposed not only by the thick walls of the *polis*, but also by his blind powerlessness to escape his isolation decreed by the autocratic Augustus. Although his fragile body remained inside the fortress, his glory transcended all obstacles and lives on today. Overcoming the confinement of the city, the crystalline sound of his lyre entered into eternity, into the conscience of future generations, into the cultural heritage of the world.

This book, far from being an exegesis or a critical effort at synthesis and analysis, is intended to reconstitute for the reader the small universe of Ovid, which will surpass the limits of some works dedicated to his life and work. I have sketched a historical portrait of

---

victory won by the conquering Roman legions against the Dacians, whose struggle for the defense of their liberty and their existence as a kingdom during the wars of A.D. 101-102 and 105-106 was led by their king, Decebal. The monument, which was first studied during the second half of the nineteenth century by Grigore Tocilescu, was restored in 1977 on the occasion of the centennial celebration of the independence of modern Romania.

Ovid, always placing him in the environment in which he lived. I have combined, perhaps more than is usual, the man with his environment, using selected information to help depict a veridical fresco of the epoch and its history.

Readers will find in the following pages elements that will help them understand the poet as reflected in his own creations. I have written this book for the purpose of enhancing the reader's understanding of Ovid's life and poetry. This book is also intended to be an introduction for the many visitors who come to Constanţa each year on holiday to visit the land where Ovid lived and wrote. Romania is a country enriched by the history of both the Geto-Dacian and Roman civilizations, and, during a time of interaction between these two civilizations, Publius Ovidius Naso dominated the shore of the Black Sea like a Prometheus.

CHAPTER 1

TOMIS AND THE BLACK SEA COAST

Any examination of Romanian literature studying the profound implications of its poetry requires a retrospective of two thousand years when, in Tomis, on the shore of Pontus Euxinus, the ancient name for the Black Sea, one could hear in Latin the elegies of two great works: *Tristia* and *Epistulae ex Ponto* by Publius Ovidius Naso. Ovid, along with other Latin poets, opened the paths to a universe of immortal creations, followed later by an entire pleiad of poets from all parts of the civilized world. Late antiquity, the Middle Ages, the Renaissance, the Modern Age, and the Contemporary Period owe tribute to Ovid and his creations of elevated inspiration.

For Romanian poetry, Ovid represents not only an artistic and literacy pinnacle, as well as a source of historical information, but he was also the bard who, at the beginning of a new era, sang to the austere souls of the Geto-Dacians. In both Romanian and world literature, Ovid has remained as a symbol of the greatest artistic and literary creation, which has kept him alive in the memory of each generation over the past two millennia.

Let us begin our study by examining the land where Ovid was sent into exile. There are few sea shores in the world that completely enjoy the generous sun and abundant sand, fine and clean, such as that of the western shore of the Black Sea. Over a distance of 245 kilometers, the length of the eastern border of Romanian Dobrogea, from Chilia on the Danube Delta, as far south as Vama Veche, a beautiful beach extends, with few interruptions, like a silver ribbon, marked by a series of resorts, hospitable oases, and health spas enjoyed by millions of people each summer.

Since the earliest times, the sun, the water, and the sand increased the possibilities for food and warmth for man, cured his illnesses, and helped him recover his strength, opening for him infinite horizons, as well as providing inspiration. The boundless surface of the sea often called him, with its hidden voice, to witness its infinity – that apparent joining of the sky with the boundless waters, just like the joining of night and day.

Beyond the strip of sand on which the foam brought by the waves dissipates, the Dobrogean plateau begins, delimited by the Danube to the north and west, and bordering the pre-Balkan plain to the south. The hills, the valleys, and the old mountains in the northwest, all with a unique geological structure, give the Romanian trans-Danubian region an intrinsic touristic potential.

If we add to this the wonderful natural environment, with its unique landscapes, a second quality, the vestiges of its rich history, we can fully understand why this region is visited each year by tourists from all over the world.

Indeed, the fertile land of Dobrogea, a land inhabited in ancient times by the Getae and Romans, and later by the Romanians, the offspring of these two ancient peoples, has been a place that has seen a succession of civilizations, in an uninterrupted evolution. From early antiquity until the present day, the people who have lived here have left everywhere traces of their work and deeds, marked in clay and stone, brick and marble, glass and metal. In this environment, spiritual manifestations of a remarkable essence took place; this was reflected in art, poetry, and literature.

Uncovered from under the earthen veil that preserved them until our time or taken from the shelves of libraries – when we speak of books – they are monuments to the greatness of previous generations, messages transmitted from the earlier centuries to us, allowing us to communicate with our ancestors, to learn about their struggles and aspirations, their faith and traditions, their wisdom and poetry, their sufferings and joys, as they truly were. Here on the shore of this hospitable sea, the muses accompanied both the anonymous bard and the poet-genius whose name became immortal.

Everywhere you look, you can see how nature and man-made creations, both past and present, unite the beautiful and the useful in a unique harmony, characteristic of the Romanian shore of the Black Sea. Here, history has been embodied in ruins of fortresses and fortifications, in stone, marble, and bronze monuments, in remnants of architecture and sculpture, all attesting to a rich multi-millennia history.

Nevertheless, between past and present there are many bridges of knowledge, which we are able to cross. Let us first look at the heart of Dobrogea, contemporary Constanța, a city with a history of over two thousand five hundred years, both to admire its most hidden historical vestiges, but also to listen to the lament of the crystalline echoes rising out of the undulating sea, in their joining with the verses created and spoken by Ovid along its shore. We shall make our way toward him, with reverence and respect because his poetry belongs to us. It is the gift offered to us two thousand years ago by history, whose muse, Clio, gave Euterpe[2] the privilege to let her lyric echoes be heard, through Ovid, as far as the land of the Getae.

***

All roads leading to the Romanian seashore, coming from any cardinal point, and especially from Ovid's native Sulmo (the Italian Abruzzi), pass through Constanța, the ancient Tomis, the adopted city of the poet. Moreover, within the city, they all lead to Independence Square, or, as the locals call it, *Ovid Square*.

Ancient Tomis – modern-day Constanța – occupied the high peninsula, with steep shores jutting out like arrows into the sea, whose winter uproar was increased by submarine currents coming from the northeast; but the quietness of the south-southwestern gulf offered ships its shallowness preferable for both fishing and nautical shelter. The ancient Greeks anchored comfortably in this gulf during this time when they were sailing the sea in great numbers (especially during the seventh and sixth centuries B.C.), looking for shelter and for people to whom they could offer artisan goods in exchange for goods produced by the native population on the fertile land which they had farmed since time immemorial (stones, first carved and later polished, prove their perennial presence in this area).

Along the hospitable shore, the sea offered the essential conditions for an advantageous commercial activity as part of the material and spiritual dialogue that had already been established in the middle of the sixth century B.C. between the foreign visitors and the native Geto-Dacians. At that time, the Geto-Dacians were at an evolutionary stage of military democracy, a society in which the

---

[2]*Euterpe* was one of the nine Muses, the goddesses of music, song, and dance. In ancient times, *Euterpe* was the Muse of lyric poetry.

tribal democracy sought and purchased luxury goods sold by the Greeks. Thus, the newcomers chose this small settlement and transformed it over time into a city. The area occupied by the inhabitants, who mixed throughout the centuries with the natives, expanded as far as the promontory, where the high, often rough shore offered shelter and safety for their settlement. Recent archeological excavations in the courtyard of St. Peter and Paul's Cathedral, near the southeastern end of the peninsula, revealed unquestionable vestiges that confirm the massive presence of Geto-Dacians in the "pre-colonial" phase of the city. The area of today's Ovid Square, where the continental part of Constanța begins, contains similar evidence. Here, at the narrowing point of the peninsula, the strata of ancient civilizations were superposed: the Geto-Dacian, Greek, Roman, Byzantine, Genoese, Ottoman, and Romanian civilizations, in their chronological succession. The archeological excavations, systematic or occasional, have revealed facts that otherwise would have remained unknown. A Greek *agora* existed here – *forum* in Latin and *piață* in Romanian – as evidenced by the great Roman edifice with a mosaic on the sea wall of the modern port. Although it dates from a later period, the third through the seventh century A.D., the construction justifies the presumption of a similar urban society, in an environment in which civic, commercial, and navigational life thrived. Tradition imposed here a true ecological unity with a complex structure but, as we have mentioned above, with a precise destination: *agora, forum, piață* – in the languages of the creators of the civilization of this place.

In modern times, Ovid Square is a reminder of the elevated spiritual and historical status of Romania's oldest city – Constanța. This is the center of the city where all roads converge. Here, the bewildered eyes of the traveler experience the joy of the end of a journey that has brought him to the halls of the museums rich in history and in front of the statue of the poet whose name has been

Ovid Square in Constanta

preserved throughout the centuries: Publius Ovidius Naso – the first bard of the Romanian lands by the sea, the author of the eternal *Metamorphoses* and *Letters from Pontus*. Let us try to unravel the mystery that envelops the bronze statue and to know him in the privacy of his unhappy life.

***

The statue was commissioned between 1883-1884 by the authorities of the city of Constanţa. It was the creation of the Italian sculptor Ettore Ferrari,[3] and was unveiled in Constanţa in 1887. The dramatic and sometimes tragic events centered around this monument over the course of more than a century since its realization, especially during World War I, represent dark and sad pages in its history.[4] Only in modern times have its tribulations ended. The statue entered definitively into the patrimonial and cultural conscience of the municipality.

But the statue itself, detached from the context of its significance, appears to the casual observer as a piece of clay molded with artistry and then immortalized in the ennobled hardness of bronze, representing "a Latin poet;" the latter, in his meditative posture, with a book in his left hand and his head supported by his right hand in which long ago he held a pen, is dressed in a draped

---

[3]Ettore Ferrari (1850-1929), an Italian sculptor of great talent who dedicated himself to memorialist creations, was not only a great artistic personality, but also prominent social-political personality. He fought for a long time next to Garibaldi and Mazzini in the struggle for the Italian national ideal. Among his most famous creations, we mention sculptures of Abraham Lincoln in Washington D.C., Giordano Bruno in Rome, Giuseppe Garibaldi in Pisa, Ion Heliade-Rădulescu in Bucharest, and Ovid in Constanţa, with an identical replica in Sulmo.

[4]Florica Postolache, "Avatarurile unei statui," in *Tomis*, vol. 2, February, 1967, p. 17.

toga which falls all the way down to his ankles. 2.60 meters tall –
much taller than the average height of a human being, respecting
certain traditional canons, the statue of the poet is placed on a
Dobrogean stone pedestal with the dimensions of 2.68 x 1.61 x 1.61
meters. The face has typical features, similar to the numerous classic
marble creations that abound in the halls of museums famous for
their ancient statuaries, such as those of the National Museum in
Athens or of the Vatican in Rome to mention only some of the most
famous.

A more profound understanding of this unique monument
placed in the modern city of Constanţa at the end of the nineteenth
century, at a time of revival, can be obtained when one reads on the
front of the pedestal, in both Latin and Romanian, the famous,
moving epitaph written by Ovid himself, in Tomis, in the manner of
the funerary verses of his time:

I, who lie here, with tender loves once played
Naso, the bard, whose life his wit betrayed.
Grudge not, o lover, as thou passest by,
A prayer: "Soft may the bones of Naso lie!"[5]

Hic ego qui iaceo tenerorum lusor amocum
Ingenio perii Naso poeta meo
At tibi qui transis ne sit grave quisquis amasti
Dicere Nasonis molliter ossa cubent.

(*Tristia*, III, 3, V, 73-76)

Nevertheless, the statue rendering Ovid meditating surpasses
the strict representation of a character of unique talent, dear to the
entire Latin race (and to humanity in general) which, from antiquity

---

[5]Ovid, *Tristia/Ex Ponto,* English translation by Arthur Leslie Wheeler, Harvard
University Press, 1996, p. 115.

until today, is indebted to his creation. Shortly after the reintegration of Dobrogea within the natural borders of the lands of the ancestors of the Romanians, more than one hundred and twenty-five years ago, the inhabitants of Constanța, led by Remus Opreanu, an ardent promoter of the Romanian spirit and of the Latin origin of the Romanians, ordered the statue of Ovid,[6] in the conception of the great Italian sculptor. The bronze statue symbolized the birth of the Romanian language and people in the Carpathian-Danubian-Pontic area and attested to the continuous presence for thousands of years on this territory of a people born from the mixture of Latin genius with Geto-Dacian heroism. It symbolized the ethnic origin of the Romanians, which was, at that time, being revealed by the archeological research in Dobrogea of Grigore Tocilescu.[7] The testimonial monument to this origin is, undoubtedly, the great triumphal monument at Adamclisi, *Tropaeum Traiani*, built in A.D. 109.

The statue of Ovid represents, therefore, because of its historical, artistic, and social significance, a symbol, an urban adornment, and, at the same time, an aureole of a people of Latin origin, present for thousands of years on this land, the creators of a civilization and beneficiary of the cultural traditions inherited from their ancestors: the Romans and the Geto-Dacians. The latter, in Ovid's vision, had the cruelties of their warlike life imprinted on

---

[6]Remus Opreanu (1844-1904), the first prefect of the county of Constanța after its reintegration within the borders of Romania. He had great administrative and organizational skills and contributed to the writing of the law for the organization of Dobrogea in 1881. He was the initiator and president of the committee to establish a statue of Ovid formed in 1883.

[7]Grigore Tocilescu (1850-1909), famous Romanian historian, archaeologist, epigraphist, and folklorist, author of the research done between 1882 and 1884 at Adamclisi (*Tropaeum Traiani*), following which, in collaboration with two Viennese scholars, he published a monograph on the monument (in Romanian and German).

their faces, but they always found, in the depths of their souls, comforting words for the exiled poet, during his bitter suffering in Tomis.

To understand further the significance of this statue it is necessary to examine Ovid's life, from his birth in Italy to his tragic end in Tomis.

CHAPTER II

OVID IN ITALY

Who was Ovid and where did he come from? What were the circumstances that drove him away from his country? These are questions we can answer by scrutinizing the distant centuries of Roman history, when social and political unrest required the establishment of an autocratic form of government, which would endure for many centuries in the form of the empire, a rare thing in the history of humanity.

The second half of the first century B.C. was characterized by the disappearance of the republican form of government in Rome and the transition to the empire. This transition took on violent forms, and to understand this process requires careful examination.

Gaius Julius Caesar, victor at Pharsalus in the year 48 B.C., eliminated his most daring adversary in the triumvirate, namely Pompeius Magnus, thus consolidating a dictatorship that would prepare his dynastic crown. Political motives that superseded his hidden aspirations determined him to be prudent and not accept it. Caesar drew up the first plan to conquer Dacia, which had reached its peak development at that time under the leadership of King Burebista, because the Geto-Dacians had aided his adversary at the battle of Pharsalus. However, there was great unrest in Rome. In addition, fear of the Geto-Dacian warriors in the area of the Danube, the Carpathians, and the Pontus Euxinus was great. This sentiment was reflected in verses from the time:

> *Oh heavenly gods, keep this madness away from me,*
> *And make it so that, should a disaster set the Dacians*
> > *and the Getae afoot,*
> *And should Rome fall, I shall remain safe.*

> *Procel hunc arcete furorem,*
> *O superi, motura Dahas ut clade Getasque,*
> *Secure me Roma cadat.[8]*

This testimony is given to us by Lucanus, a Latin poet who lived in Nero's time, in his famous epos *Pharsalia*, in which he expresses his fear of the people that lived in the area of the Carpathians and the Danube and who Cato the Elder knew well, with all of their characteristics.

In the year 44 B.C., the last great triumvir, Caesar, was removed from the arena of events with his body bleeding from stab wounds inflicted by the conspirators, led by Brutus and Cassius, the last fanatical defenders of the decaying senatorial republic.

That same year, King Burebista, the creator of the first centralized and independent Dacian state, met his end while he was preparing to confront his powerful adversary. It is possible that right in Argedava,[9] the capital of his kingdom, the conspirators of the aristocracy – the *Tarabostes* –, driven by their passion for power and fear of conflict with their powerful neighbor, assassinated their king,

---

[8]Lucanus, *Pharsalia*, II, 295-297.

[9]*Dicţionar de istorie veche a României*, Bucureşti, 1976. See *Argedava*.

preferring a disgraceful peace to freedom through a heroic fight, on the grounds of a pretended friendship with Rome.

But fate charted a different course.

In Rome, the aristocracy could no longer recover the virtues of their ancestors, which would have helped it rebuild the republic. Thus, with the violent disappearance of the dictator, a series of struggles began that allowed for the establishment of autocratic leadership, known to history as the Empire of Augustus. In his will, Caesar named Gaius Octavianus, his nephew by his sister, as his legal heir. Swarthy, young, and almost beardless, the new pretender to power proved himself capable, tactful, and persevering. He took advantage of favorable circumstances to eliminate gradually all of his adversaries who were watching him from the loftiness of their authority and equivocal experience.

During his long reign, the borders of the empire expanded considerably. The foundations of the empire had not yet been laid when, in the Lower Danube region, the Geto-Dacian tribes, who earlier had been part of the centralized and independent Dacian state of Burebista, became increasingly hostile toward each other at the instigation of the proconsul of Macedonia, Marcus Licinius Crassus, who applied the principle of divide and conquer. Attacked by the Dacians and the Bastarns, the Thracian tribe of the Denteleti managed to drive away their enemies with the support of the legions of Crassus. The Denteleti also had the support of Roles, a Geto-Dacian chieftain in the southwest of Dobrogea, emphatically entitled "friend and ally of the Roman people."

Other chieftains in the Lower Danube, namely Dapyx and Zyraxes, the latter with his capital at Genucla,[10] were defeated after

---

[10] *Ibidem.*

fierce resistance and subjected to Roman domination. This
domination was exercised indirectly, through the Odrysii tribe of
Thracians who posted their garrisons in the Dacian fortresses on the
right bank of the Danube.

The Greek commercial fortresses on the shore of the Pontus
Euxinus preferred an alliance with Rome to avoid conflicts with the
Geto-Dacians, the Bastarns, and the Sarmatians, and to maintain
their traditional commercial advantages under the protecting shield
of a great power. Already in the first years of their presence in this
part of the world, the Romans established the *Praefectura orae
maritimae[11]* – the military command of the shore – with a fleet that
permanently protected the coast, along with the traditional Greek
fortresses, commanded by the proconsul of Macedonia. Among
those who held this post at the beginning of the new era were Vestalis
and Lucius Pomponius Flaccus. The headquarters of the prefect's
office was located in Tomis, the best and most strategic port.

Assisted at first by skillful supporters, such as Agrippa[12] and
Maecenas,[13] the former a great general and collaborator of the
emperor, the latter, a political man and supporter of the writers of the
time, Octavius Augustus began his work as a leader glorifying it with
the magnificence of an epoch of authentic cultural value, represented
by a true pleiad of poets: Catullus, Virgil, Horace, Tibullus, Ovid,

---

[11]*Ibidem.*

[12]Marcus Vipsanius Agrippa (63-12 B.C.), one of the main generals of
Augustus, whose name is linked to important campaigns and buildings in Rome
(the pantheon, aqueducts, thermae, etc.)

[13]Gaius Cilnius Maecenas (70-8 B.C.), an important personality of political and
literary life at the end of the old era; a wealthy man, he supported, materially
and morally, the most remarkable poets and prose writers of the time, including
Virgil, Horace, and Propertius – while he also proved to be a skillful writer
himself. By extension, his name became synonymous with a supporter and
protector of the arts.

Propertius,[14] and many others. Also at this time, the historian Titus Livius[15] distinguished himself, a great personality whose work has remained valuable throughout the two thousand years since its elaboration. Leadership now firmly in the hands of Octavian and his wife Livia – as authoritative and ambitious as she was skilled in the art of diplomacy – a climate favorable to artistic creation thrived in Rome. Literary circles were established, which represented permanent sources of artistic creation. Among these, we mention those of Maecenas, M. Valerius Messala Corvinus, and Asinius Pollio.[16] The artistic activities that made many Roman citizens – most of whom were aristocrats – forget about politics materialized in the impressive achievements of urban planning, and poetical creations, driven by the critical exigency of the literary circles previously mentioned, which enhanced cultural life through public readings.[17]

No document from the time mentions the birth of Ovid, with the exception of his creations written in exile, in which we find testimonies of an autobiographical character (*Tristia*, IV, 10, 3-5) which we can easily corroborate with the historical events of the epoch and the picturesque natural environment of Sulmo.

Publius Ovidius Naso was born on 20 March 43 B.C., in the city of *Sulmo* – today's Sulmona – in the region of the Abruzzi Mountains in central Italy, 158 kilometers from Rome, located along the road that connected the eternal fortress to the city on the coast of the Adriatic Sea, Pescara. It was the time of the holidays called

---

[14] *Scriitori greci şi latini*, Bucureşti, 1978, passim.

[15] *Ibidem.*

[16] *Ibidem.*

[17] I. Maşkim, *Istoria Romei antice.*

Quinquatrii,[18] dedicated to the goddess Minerva, to whom Ovid would later express his poetical gratitude (*Fasti*, V, 833-834).

Very common at the time were the heated disputes caused by political ambitions unbridled after the death of Caesar, when the protagonists of the second triumvirate tested their arms on the battlefield – the battle of Mutina between the armies of Marcus Antonius and those of the Senate, commanded by Octavian, had just come to an end.

> *There first I saw the light, and if thou wouldst know the date,*
> *'Twas when both consuls fell under stress of like fate.*[19]

> *Editus his ego sum, nee non, ut tempora noris,*
> *Cum cecidit fato consul uterque pari.*

> (*Tristia*, IV, 10, 5-6)

Mentioning the name of his city of birth, the poet completes the information with the geographical detail rendered in a soft poetic color:

> *Sulmo is my native place, a land rich in ice-cold streams,*
> *Thrice thirty miles from the city.*[20]

> *Sulmo mihi patria est, gelidis uberrimus undis,*
> *Milia qui novies distat ab urbe decem.*

> (*Tristia*, IV, 10, 3-4)

Thus, although his poetry is tributary to imagination, it offers real information regarding the time and place of his birth, with specific details that eliminate any possibility of misinterpretation.

---

[18]*Ibidem.*

[19]Ovid, *Tristia*, p. 197.

[20]*Ibidem.*

The image of the city of Sulmo, in the land of the Pelignis, "rich in green pastures, with herds of sheep, with cool springs, with fertile fields and groves of olive trees and almond trees, and especially its countless vineyards," described so vividly in his work, will persist in the memory of the poet all his life, even during his exile in Scythia Minor.

Ovid came from a family of lesser nobles. His parents did not have a great fortune, but they wanted to give their two children – Ovid and his older brother, Lucius – an education equal to that received by aristocratic children, to enable their ascension into the hierarchy of public officials – *cursus honorum*. To develop their patriotism, their father would often recount to them episodes from the glorious history of the Romans, from the past of the tribe of the Pelignis, from which they descended, as well as of the city of Sulmo, where they had been born, assuring them that its founder was the legendary Solymus, a brother-in-arms of the Trojan Aeneas.[21]

After he had acquired the first elements of education from his parents – *me docuere parentes* – as well as in the local school – *ludus* – the son of the Sulmonian noble was sent to Rome, together with his brother, in the care of a *grammaticus*, to learn orthography, grammar, and the Greek language; afterwards, parting with the *toga praetexta*, he put on the *toga virilis* – as a sign of manhood – an event that took place between the years 28 and 26 B.C.:

> *We brothers assumed the toga of a freer life*
> *And our shoulders put on the broad stripe of purple*
> *While still our pursuits remained as before.*[22]

---

[21]Nicolae Lascu, *Ovidiu, omul și poetul*, Editura Dacia, Cluj, 1971, p. 14.

[22]Ovid, *Tristia*, p. 199.

Liberior fratri sumpta mihique toga est,
Induiturque umeris cum lato purpura clavo,
Et studium nobis, quod fuit ante, manet.

(*Tristia*, IV, 10, 28-30)

Afterwards, the two brothers from Sulmo attended the school of rhetoric – frequented by the younger members of wealthy families – where they acquired the art of oratory under the auspices of famous professors like Porcius Latro and Aurelius Fuscus.

> *While still of tender age we began our training and*
> > > *through our father's care*
> *We came to attend upon men of the city distinguished in*
> > > *the liberal arts.*[23]

Protinus excolimur teneri curaque parentis,
Imus ad insignes Urbis ab arte viros.

(*Tristia*, IV, 10, 15-16)

The influence of the rhetorical arts, greatly cultivated in that epoch, would be felt in many of Ovid's creations. The accusation that the poet is tributary, in his verses, to the exaggerations specific to the oratorical arts, is contradicted by the incontestable truth that there is a unique structural unity between the form and substance of the poet's thinking.

> ...the question of the influence of rhetoric in Ovid's work cannot be limited exclusively to an analysis of the form. More important is the human, psychological, and fantastical substance of the content. That is why we may rather talk of an influence and an impulse that acted in depth, nourishing some inborn tendencies of the poet, of a free and organic relation,

---

[23] *Ibidem.*

manifested through fundamental and substantial tendencies and attitudes in the nature and art of the poet. Thus, it is to rhetorical declamations that Ovid owes the exuberant passion of some of the discourses in *Metamorphoses*, as well as the modern complexity in the psychological analyses.[24]

After attending courses at this school, Lucius, Ovid's older brother, was attracted by the oratorical duels in the Forum:

My brother's bent even in the green of years was oratory:
He was born for the stout weapons of the wordy forum.[25]

Frater ad eloquium viridi tendebat ab aevo,
Fortia verbosi natus ad arma fori.

(*Tristia*, IV, 10, 17-18)

Ovid's calling, however, was poetry, which he began to cultivate with passion and talent.

Whatever I tried to write was verse.[26]

Et quod temptabam scriber versus erat

(*Tristia*, IV, 10, 26)

His passion for poetry would soon bring him fame. The young Ovid, gifted with an unbridled imagination, was convinced of his glory. But we aim to portray his sad evolution, without which the two lyrical monuments, written during his exile in Tomis, *Tristia* and *Epistulae ex Ponto*, would never have been created.

In the year 25 B.C., when Ovid turned 18 years old, to complete his intellectual formation, which in the mind of his father meant

---

[24]Nicolae Lascu, *Ovidiu, omul și poetul*, pp. 26-27.

[25]Ovid, *Tristia*, p. 199.

[26]*Ibidem.*

oratory with all the advantages that it could bring, he was sent to learn and study Hellenic culture in Greece, Asia Minor, and Sicily, regions with an ancient Greek historical and cultural tradition, which were part of the extra-Italic structure of the Roman Empire of the time. During his Mediterranean journey, Ovid's brother died. Upon his return, to avoid disappointing his parents who hoped he would pursue a more practical career, he joined the Roman juridical practice, occupying various positions, among them that of *triumvir capitalis* – supervisor of public order in the city, and afterwards that of judge:

> *Nor was fate of those on trial wrongfully entrusted to me,*
> *Suits to be examined by centumvirs.*[27]

> *Nec male commisa est nobis fortuna reorum*
> *Lisque decem deciens inspicienda viris.*

(Tristia, II, 93-94)

As a judge – *decemvir litibus iudicandis* – Ovid tried to interpret *leges Iuliae de adulteriis* decreed by Augustus for the support of Roman aristocratic families, which were manifesting ever more numerous and undesirable signs of disintegration.[28] But, applied according to Ovid's view, these laws were aimed first of all at the imperial family, with its many examples of moral degradation. Finding himself unequipped with judicial sense and probably not wanting to venture on dangerous professional grounds, the poet no

---

[27] *Ibidem*, p. 63.

[28] Among the laws concerning the family and marriage, through which Augustus was trying to end debauchery, conjugal libertinage, and infidelity, and to thus strengthen society and reestablish the once austere morals and manners, an important place was held by the *leges Iuliae de adulteriis coercendis*, stipulating very severe sanctions. Of the same importance was *lex de maritandis ordinibus* and *lex Papia Poppea*, the latter differentiating between a bachelor and married people without children.

longer ran for the magistracy, renouncing his *laticlava* – a toga with the wide purple ribbon – worn by those who held this superior dignity, resigning himself to wearing the *augusticlava*.[29] He was no longer attracted to this career that implied agitation and a fighting spirit, as we find out from his own writings:

> *...I narrowed my purple stripe:*
> *That was a burden too great for my powers.*
> *I had neither a body to endure the toil nor a mind suited*
> > *to it.[30]*

> *...clavi mensura coacta est :*
> *Maius erat nostris viribus illud onus.*
> *Nec patiens corpus, nec mens fuit apta labori.*

> > (*Tristia*, IV, 10, 34-37).

In accordance with the matrimonial arrangements made by his parents, the young poet married, but, for unknown reasons, his first marriage lasted only a short time:

> *When I was scarce more than a boy a wife unworthy*
> > *and unprofitable*
> *Became mine – mine for but a short space.[31]*

> *Paene mihi puero nec digna utilis uxor.*
> *Est data, quae tempus per breve nupta fuit.*

> > (*Tristia*, IV, 10, 69-70)

---

[29]See the dictionaries.

[30]Ovid, *Tristia*, p. 199.

[31]*Ibidem*, p. 203.

It appears, according to his verses, that his first wife was to blame for their separation. Further, he appreciates his second wife, but this marriage did not last either:

> Into her place came one, blameless,
> But not destined to remain my bride.[32]

> Illi successit, quamvis sine crimine coniunx,
> Non tamen in nostro firma futura toro.

(*Tristia*, IV, 10, 71-72)

Why did he divorce his second wife as well, if, as he admits himself, she was a decent woman? Since Ovid does not want to explain, we must respect his discretion and continue his biography. After two failed attempts, he married again. His third wife, Fabia, met his expectations, being as faithful as Ulysses's Penelope, and standing by him during difficult times:

> And last is she who remained with me till the twilight
>   of my declining years,
> Who has endured to be the mate of an exile husband.[33]

> Ultima, quae mecum seros permansit in annos,
> Sustinuit coniux exulit esse viri.

(*Tristia*, IV, 10, 73-74)

This time the poet offers us a more complete presentation of his last wife: Fabia came from "the land of the Faliscs, rich in orchards" and belonged to an aristocratic family. She was loved by her husband, who recognized her superior qualities. Moreover, she took her devotion beyond ordinary limits, wishing to follow her husband into exile. But, having a sense of great dignity, the poet did not accept

---

[32] *Ibidem.*   Those left @ home.

[33] *Ibidem.*

this. He considered that he should endure alone the punishment that he received for his personal errors.

In his autobiographical elegy, Ovid also tells us that he had a daughter and that she gave him two grandsons:

My daughter, twice fertile, but not of one husband,
In her early youth made me grandsire.[34]

Filia me mea bis prima fecunda iuventa
Sed non ex uno coniuge, fecit avum.

(*Tristia*, IV, 10, 75-76)

At the moment of his dramatic departure into exile, his daughter was in Africa with her family, as we find out from the famous elegy: "The last night in Rome."

My daughter was far separated from us on the shores
                                        of Libya,
And we could not inform her of my fate.[35]

Nata procul Libycis aberat diversa sub oris,
Nec poterat fati certitor esse mei.

(*Tristia*, I, 3, 19-20)

Undoubtedly, the absence of his daughter added to the pain of the dramatic moment. And, for a more complete picture of the somber disintegration of his family, the poet reminds us of the premature death of his brother Lucius, whom he had loved dearly:

---

[34] *Ibidem.*

[35] *Ibidem.*

And now my brother had seen but twice ten years of life
When he passed away, and thenceforth I was bereft
                                    of half myself.[36]

Iamque decem vitae frater geminaverat annos,
Cum perit, et coepi parte carere mei.

(*Tristia*, IV, 10, 32-33)

Once he completes the portrayal of his family tragedy, the poet draws attention in his autobiographical poems to his personal drama. He makes us impartial spectators to the process of his artistic evolution, appearing to want to establish the errors that he committed (which, when judged objectively, did not include anything that – later on – would have been considered a terrible crime in the imperial house).

Like his other famous fellow poets, as a young male he began frequenting the literary circles in Rome. As Virgil and Horace enjoyed the protection of Maecenas, Ovid found support in the person of Marcus Valerius Messala Corvinus, to whom he would later express his gratitude. There, Ovid let himself be attracted by the world of letters. He felt the fascinating climate suited him and began to learn the art of writing poetry, to which, ever since his adolescence, he had felt an irresistible attraction.

Living during the age of Augustus, whose liberty he enjoyed to the full, the poet admired, without critical restriction, contemporary Roman writers, some of them serving him as models:

The poets of that time I fondly reverenced:
All bards I thought so many present gods.
Oft times Maced, already advanced in years,
Read to me of the birds he loved,

---

[36] *Ibidem.*

Of noxious snakes and healing plants.
Oft times Propertius would declaim his flaming verse
By right of the comradeship that joined him to me.
Ponticus famed in epic, Bassus also, famed in iambics,
Were pleasant members of that friendly circle.
And Horace of the many rhythms held in thrall our ears
While he attuned his fine-wrought songs to the
                                         Ausonian lyre.[37]

Temporis illius colui fovique poëtas,
Quotque aderant vates, rebar adesse deos.
Saepe suas volucres legit mihi grandior aevo,
Quaeque nocet serpens, quae iuvat herba, Macer,
Saepe suos solitus recitare Propertills ignes,
Iure sodalicii, quo mihi iunctus erat.
Ponticus heroo, Bassus quoque clarus iambis
Dulcia convictus membra fuere mei.
Et tenuit nostras numerosus Horatius aures,
Dum ferit Ausonia carmina culta lyra.

(*Tristia*, IV, 10, 41-50)

In Rome, the poetic universe of Ovid was circumscribed to a personal area, to never before examined paths of human sensibility; it reveals a new range of emotional states specific to a protean personality in its artistic ascension and in permanent movement from the diverse themes that it proposes to realize poetically. The different stages in Ovid's creation can be reconstituted with some exactness, as we follow their ascending line, from facile to difficult, namely from the gallant products of the collections of his youth – *Amores, Ars amandi* – with their subtle eroticism, to *Metamorphoses*, a work that is as grave as it is complex, and to the elaboration of *Tristia* and

---

[37]*Ibidem*, p. 201.

Epistulae ex Ponto, testimonies of his seclusion, meant to give tonality to a new literary form that would be cultivated centuries later.

In the first stage of his poetic creation, Ovid was a "playful poet of tender love" (*tenerorum lusor amorum*), as he later described himself several times (*Tristia*, IV, 10, 1; III, 3, 73). The poems, which came to him very easily during this period of his formation, gathered in the collections *Amores*, *Heroides*, *Ars amandi*, and *De medicamine faciei femineae*, combine sensibility with mundane subtlety, details of everyday life with references to mythological equivalences, all these in a pleasant form, often manifested. In fact, Ovid did not intend from the beginning to transmit to his contemporary or future readers a lyrical confession about his personal feelings, as does Catullus[38] who tells about his love for Lesbia, or Propertius about his love for Cynthia. Ovid always tends to go beyond the sphere of personal feelings, transposing love, as source of poetry, to a plan of general ideas. Thus, in his poems with love themes we will not find Ovid as a character of reference, but rather the youth of his time. He educates them in his way, intending to initiate them in the art of beneficial love. He warns them almost solemnly of the ill-fated consequences of unreturned love, teaching them a certain code of behavior.

Ovid dedicated himself to poetry, reading some of his poems in public, participating in literary meetings, and publishing his first collection of poems that would captivate the interest of the patricians with their elegance. He planned a *Gigantomachia* (Jupiter, vanquisher of the giants), a poem in which he was going to present, in allegorical form, Augustus defeating his enemies. But he did not succeed in realizing this project. As he was at an age when the young

---

[38]*Scriitori greci şi latini*, see Catul.

imagination dashes without much judgement toward a certain lady of his choice, he used his talent to praise the woman represented conventionally, in the fashion of the Alexandrian poets, by a certain Corina:

> *When first I read my youthful songs in public,*
> *My beard had been cut but once or twice.*
> *My genius had been stirred by her who was sung*
> *throughout the city,*
> *Whom I called, not by her real name, Corina.*[39]

> *Carmina cum primum populo iuvenalia legi,*
> *Barba resecta mihi bisve semelve fuit.*
> *Moverat ingenium totam cantata per urbem*
> *Nomine non vero dicta Corinna mihi.*

(Tristia, IV, 10, 57-60)

The creations of the poet deserve exact references. *Amores* was the work through which the poet made his resounding debut in Rome. At first made up of five books, it was later reduced to three. It consists of fifty-one erotic elegies, probably written between the years 25-20 B.C., in the manner of Tibullus[40] and Propertius, dedicated to Corina.

The poet in these poems is not the same as the one in *Tristia* and *Epistulae ex Ponto*, in which the lyricism is projected from personal feelings. Here he considers himself as a starting point, in an effort to make love a common possession of the entire Roman youth, whom he understood profoundly and loved dearly. The goals he set for himself contained nothing impure or corrupting. Nevertheless, the eroticism he manifested in his poems contravened republican

---

[39]Ovid, *Tristia*, p. 201.

[40]*Ibidem.*

puritanism, for which the poet was supposed to show respect in order to be accepted, not only by the youth, but also by the elders. Almost all the elegies in this collection denote sensibility, love having a facile character. Ovid sees Corina with the eyes of the aesthete, who knows how to appreciate a living sculpture, but does not communicate to it the passion of the great lovers of the literature of this genre, such as Dante, Petrarch, or the Romanian poet Mihai Eminescu did later on.

Nevertheless, the domain of the delicate nature is harmoniously interwoven with that of art, a phenomenon lacking passionate vibrations. Even so, love treated at an aesthetic level in *Amores* seems attainable for everyone; every young man struck by Cupid's arrow finds himself in it:

> Every lover is a soldier, and Cupid has a camp of his own;
> Atticus, believe me, every lover is a soldier.[41]

> Militat omnis amans et habet sua castra Cupido;
> Attice, crede mihi, militat omnis amans.

> (*Amores*, I, 9, 1-2)

Although the first literary products of Ovid reveal that his path to major art was a long one, already at that time his creative resources made him aware of his value and gave him the certainty that his work would bring him glory.

> ...but my quest is glory through all the years,
> To be ever known in song throughout the earth.[42]

---

[41]Ovid, *Amores*, translated by Grant Showerman, revised by G.P. Gould, Harvard University Press, 1996, p. 355.

[42]*Ibidem*, p. 377.

...mihi fama perennis
Quaeritur, in toto semper ut orbe canar.

(*Amores*, I, 15, 7-8)

Further on, the Horatian *non omnis moriar* – "I shall not completely perish" – appears in his writings as well, but carrying a graver note:

I, too, when the final fires have eaten up my frame,
Shall still live on, and the great part of me survive
                                                    my death. [43]

Ergo etiam, cum me supremus adederit ignis,
Vivam, parsque mei multa superstes erit.

(*Amores*, I, 15, 41-42)

Heroides, Ovid's work of the next period, differs from *Amores* both in tonality, as well as through its dramatic passionate expression. In his first cycle of "epistles," written in elegiac distichs, the poet uses the rhetorical style that he learned from his masters – Aurelius Fuscus and Porcius Latro. The subjects and the characters were borrowed from various sources: Homer's poems, Greek tragedies, and the national epos of the Romans (*Aeneid*). The use of these themes, of common places, proves the vast erudition of Ovid, with deep implications of a mythological and literary nature, an erudition that would be confirmed by his work of maturity, *Metamorphoses*. The heroines, Penelope, Dido, Medea, Phaedra, as they are brought to life in *Heroides*, appear animated to incandescence by a never dying passion. Although they populate the contents of epistles, they relive the dramas of the legends, with their

---

[43] *Ibidem*, p. 379.

unbridled love, as is the case of Phaedra, or with the paroxysmal hatred of Medea:

> *But now, what I am to fear I know not – yet none the less*
> *I fear*
> *all things, distraught,*
> *And wide is the field lies open for my cares.*[44]

> *Quid timeam ignoro timeo lamen omnia demens:*
> *Et patet in curas area lata meas.*

(Heroides, I, 71-72)

The poet emphasizes the character of Medea, taken from the tragedy of the same name written by Euripides and from *Argonautica* of Apollonius of Rhodes.[45] Ovid's preoccupation with this woman, unique in the literature of the time, is revealed by his tragedy, *Medea*,[46] written in his youth and which, unfortunately, was lost (although it is possible that he never wrote it). The sorrow of Medea, caused by the news that the man she loves, Jason, is marrying Creusa, whirls wildly and reaches the point of self-denial, of dementia.

Another type of heroine appears in *Heroides IV* and is borrowed from Virgil's *Aeneid*. She is Dido,[47] evoked in the trying situation when Aeneas is preparing to leave her for Lavinia. Next to this loving woman, saddened at her abandonment by Aeneas, we mention Homer's heroine, Penelope,[48] the prototype of conjugal fidelity, as wise as her husband Ulysses was inventive, but also cunning. And

---

[44]Ovid, *Heroides/Amores*, translated by Grant Showerman, revised by G.P. Gould, Harvard University Press, 1996, p. 17.

[45]*Scriitori greci și latini…*, see Apollonios din Rodos.

[46]Anca Balaci, *op. cit.*, see Medea.

[47]*Ibidem.*

[48]*Ibidem.*

after the author of the *Heroides* honors these two types of virtuous women, he presents Phaedra,[49] the woman who was torn by consuming passion for Hippolytus, the son of her husband. This heroine breaks the laws of nature and morality and sets free her unbridled carnal passions, causing horror and disapproval amongst sensible people. The *Heroides* represent a model of artistic perfection and at the same time they show the author as a fine connoisseur of the human soul.

Ars amandi (or *Ars amatoria*), composed of three books and finished in the year 2 B.C., is a true practical manual of erotica, a monumental catechism of love.

The poet – we do not know to what purpose – had the ambition of becoming the preceptor of the youth, their guide on the sinuous roads of Eros:

> *Should anyone here in Rome lack finesse at love-making,*
> > *let him*
> *Try me – read my book, and results are guaranteed.*[50]
>
> *Si quis in hoc artem populo non novit amandi*
> *Me legal et lecto carmine doctus amet.*

(*Ars amandi*, I, 1-2)

The didactic tendency which, beginning already with *Amores*, becomes recurrent in Ovid's work, now manifests itself in many nuances.

In the first book, Ovid speaks of how to choose and seduce a woman. In the second book, he teaches the art of keeping one's lady

---

[49] *Ibidem.*

[50] Ovid, *The Erotic Poems*, translated with an introduction and notes by Peter Green Penguin Books, 1982, chapter "The Art of Love," Book I, p. 166.

love. In the third book, he instructs his women students, giving them advice as to how they should behave to become worthy of being loved. These themes confirm the purpose of his work, but they do not annihilate its lyricism, because, we must not forget, this meticulous manual for the use of young people – as Ovid intended it – was written by a poet.

Preeminently mundane, Ovid describes the meeting places of young people – theaters, circus shows, and the forum. He depicts aspects of everyday life, sartorial details, etc. Moreover, he is concerned with matters of personal hygiene and gives young people advice in this respect of a discrete precision, motivated with ingenuity. The third book is dedicated in its entirety to women, teaching them the art of appeal by emphasizing their physical and spiritual qualities. They need to know when and how to laugh or cry, how to acquire that *quid femineum*, "feminine something." As in his previous writings, the poet proves himself a connoisseur of the female psychology.

Through his nature and especially by cultivating his lyrical-didactic literary genre, Ovid proves himself a man of his time. He is not a *laudator temporis acti* – admirer of the past – like Virgil; rather, he sings of the present, rejoicing at the prosperous century:

> *Let others worship the past; I much prefer the present,*
> *Am delighted to be alive today.*[51]

> *Prisca iuvent alios: ego me nunc denique natum*
> *Gratulator; haec aetas moribus apta meis.*

>   (*Ars amatoria*, III, 121-122).

---

[51]Ovid, *The Erotic Poems*, chapter "The Art of Love," Book III, p. 217.

Thus, he does not withdraw into the past, nor does he long nostalgically for a world that has ceased to exist. Instead, he reproduces a living reality, making common cause with it. It is important to draw to the attention of those people who try to escape into a timeless zone that the declaration of Ovid can serve them as a civic model at the times when, for whatever reasons, they adopt a negative attitude toward the only certain reality: the present.

The author does not dislike the past, but the only thing he takes from it is a collection of examples and lessons to understand even better the century he lives in. He does not aim to find an opportunity for contemplative withdrawal in the evocations of the past.

The poet still had a long way to go before he reached the elevated poetry of his contemporaries, Virgil, Horace, and the other great poets of Rome, whose friendship he cultivated with care. Despite this, the first objective of the candidate for public glory was achieved: he won over the young aristocratic generation. The poet was happy and continued to write ardently, completing a new work.

It was a time when Ovid frequented more and more often the literary circle centered around Messala Corvinus. He befriended the great elegist Propertius, he saw Virgil, and became enchanted with the lyre of Horace, whose work remained the focus of his admiration throughout his entire life. Certainly, the poetry of his great predecessors is situated on different thematic coordinates; his contact with these consecrated poets would influence him for the better, but only during the following period. He continued to write poems dedicated to unimportant subjects. He went on writing mundane poetry, of gallantry, often followed by frivolity, addressed to the aristocratic youth, who would be overcome with joy. Ovid was content, he enjoyed a wide popularity, reaped the laurels that were given to him everywhere, and, thus encouraged, continued to write superficial works, sometimes reduced to simple boudoir advises and, in any case, below the level of serious art. We mention in this sense *De medicamine faciei femineae – On Facial Treatments for Ladies*, a true cosmetics treatise, and *Remedia amoris – Cures for Love*, in which the author, from the loftiness of his aura, gives advice to young people touched by the passion of love, not to fall into despair.

It goes without saying that *De medicamine faciei femineae* contributed a great deal to his popularity among his female admirers, but not to his achieving prestige as a great poet. The treatise contains, especially in its introductory part, realistic observations, reflections of a world of luxurious interiors, useful ideas, as well as a real talent for penetrating the feminine soul. Women must maintain purity in both their physical, as well as their interior aspects:

> *Your first concern, girls, should be proper behaviour:*
> *With a fine personality, features are sure to please.*[52]

> *Prima sit in vobis morum tutela, puellae:*
> *Ingenio facies conciliante placet.*

(*De medicamine faciei*, 43-44)

In his early work, the poet cannot be accused of corrupting morals. Rather, he can be identified as a profound connoisseur of the sensitive feminine soul. As an argument in favor of this appreciation, we cite the admiration of the poet for the *agrestic* simplicity of women in former times:

> *Those old-time Sabine women,*
> *Under the early kings, may have chosen to cultivate*
> *Their fathers' fields, not their own persons: when the*
> > *red-cheeked*
> *Matron in her high chair was forever spinning yarn*

---

[52]Ovid, *The Erotic Poems*, chapter "On Facial Treatment for Ladies," p. 265.

With calloused thumb, when the lambs her daughter
pastured
She would pen herself, herself heap twigs and logs
On the family hearth.[53]

Forsitan antiquae, Tatio sub rege, Sabinae
Maluerint, quam se, rum paterna coli.
Cum matrona premens altum rubicunda sedile,
Assiduo durum, pollice nebat opus.
Ipsaque claudebat, quos filia paverit, agnos:
Ipsa dahat virgas caesaque ligna foco.

(De medicamine faciei, 11-16)

In the verses quoted above, the poet portrays a Sabine woman. However, despite the homage brought to the rural housewife, it goes without saying that cosmetic advises would not have been much use to her. They were only intended to benefit the women contemporary with Ovid.

Chronologically, the last part of the erotic poems is the *opuscule* entitled *Remedia amoris – Cures for Love.* A hostile attitude toward love was far removed from him. Nevertheless, he felt that it was his duty to warn his admirers about situations when love is not shared or has harmful consequences.

To those suffering from erotic melancholy, he recommends physical activities, which invigorate the body and bring peace to the soul. In connection with these recommendations, he praises life in the countryside, with its simple but healthy joys, portraying an authentic rural picture; we do not exaggerate when we say that these verses can be placed rightfully next to Virgil's *Georgics*:

---

[53] Ovid, *The Erotic Poems*, chapter "On Facial Treatment for Ladies," p. 264.

What else diverts the mind? Country matters, good

                                                      farming –
These can oust all other concerns.
Tame and yoke oxen, set them to ploughing, make them
Force the share through hard soil;
Bury your seed-corn in the upturned furrow, coax your
Land into yielding a bumper crop.[54]

Rura quoque oblectant animos studiumque colendi;
Quaelibet huic curae cedere cura potest.
Colla iube domitos oneri supponere tauros.
Sanciet ut duram vomer aduncus humum.
Obrue versata Cerealia semina terra,
Quae tibi cum multo foenore reddat ager.

(*Remedia amoris*, 169-174)

Remedia amoris, which we shall present only briefly, remains an insignificant part of Ovid's erotic poetry.

The phenomenon illustrated in the works quoted above can be explained through the way of thinking specific to the early days of the empire, and, if today we wonder how was it possible for these opuses in total disagreement with the interests of a great poet to appear, we can be sure that, considering the customs of the epoch, it was in perfect harmony with the views of the Roman nobility. But Octavian Augustus, the most prominent figure of the ruling class, who still maintained the memory of the republic of Cato the Censor, did not share this opinion.[55] The emperor realized that Roman society faced the moral disintegration of the family and, consequently, adopted measures intended to reinvigorate aristocratic society. This is why the works that Ovid, written during the first part of his life,

---

[54]Ovid, *The Erotic Poems*, chapter "Cures for Love," p. 244.

[55]*Scriitori greci și latini...*, see Cato cel Bătrân.

contravened with the politics of Augustus. The poet perceived the danger and, now a mature man of forty-five years, he immediately changed his direction toward more serious art, writing *Metamorphoses*, a work of erudition consisting of fifteen books, and *Fasti*. Still, his writings on more or less free love remained irrefutable witnesses for the prosecution when their author was brought to trial. The literary cycle of erotic poems which had begun in 23 B.C. was concluded in A.D. 2, when Ovid began to write his great artistic creations, as he had announced in the last elegy of *Amores*. He began to reveal his true genius in *Metamorphoses*, written between the years A.D. 2 and 8, in which the poet proved himself to be robust, serious, tender, and inventive.

Studying the poet's sources of inspiration for this work, we discover that mythology was foremost. Effortlessly, his rich imagination peopled the land of fantasy with heroes from the world of legends, with gods, demigods, fairies, and naiads, all of whom he subjected to an endless protean process. As in the age of Augustus the evolutionist concept did not exist, the poet, following practiced beliefs, was an advocate of instantaneous transformations. Thus, in his conception of the world, there was room for his extraordinary *Metamorphoses* to come to life. By addressing this subject, Ovid may have intended to accomplish two things: to prove to the emperor that he also belonged to the group of poets who had engaged themselves in supporting him in his politics of promoting good morals in Rome, and to realize his masterpiece, considering his preference for the miraculous. These are the psychological motivations for *Metamorphoses*, the poem that represents the crowning achievement of Ovid's literary activity in Rome. In more than twelve thousand verses, the poet presents two hundred and forty-six legends, beginning with the original chaos and concluding with the apotheosis of Augustus. They are proof of true literary craftsmanship. Their value has been confirmed with the passing of time, over more than two thousand years, during which they have not lost their initial splendor. Moreover, they enriched immensely the area of imagination of later poets. Although it would appear that the sources that provided the poet with his material are not of interest, the attention stirred by the appearance of the wonderful poet from Sulmo determined literary historians to search for the sources that inspired the fifteen books. This problem of poetic genesis has been answered only partially. A complete explanation has yet to be formulated. We can state, however, with certainty that the poet was familiar with the works of a mythological character of his Greek and Latin predecessors: *Theogeny* by Hesiod, *Aitia* by Callimachus, *Heteroiumena* by Nicandor of Colophonus, *Metamorphoses* by Parthenius, the poem *The Wedding of Peleus and the Goddess Thetis* by Catullus, etc.[56]

The Greco-Roman mythological fund represents the common product of Mediterranean antiquity, accumulated since the earliest times, within the framework of the polytheistic concept of supernatural powers. In the epoch of Octavian Augustus, this mythological fund was still preserved. Mythology was no longer a religion proper, but rather a treasury of the syncretism to which people still paid respect, but not out of superstitious fear. The above-mentioned poets, including Ovid, resorted to this mythological fund. The poets of the time met on this favorable ground, competing in their artistic transformation of this rich material. It is therefore clear that, in writing his splendid *Metamorphoses*, Ovid did not imitate anyone, but instead he gathered material from this fund, his work representing a personal creation and also the apogee of his poetical art.

---

[56]Catul, *Poezii*, Editura pentru literature universal, Bucureşti, 1969, pp. 102-112 (Poem LXIV).

The poem begins solemnly with an invocation to the gods – a traditional device found in Greco-Roman poems and epics:

> *My intention is to tell of bodies changed*
> *To different forms; the gods, who made the changes,*
> *Will help me – or I hope so – with a poem*
> *That runs from the world's beginning to our own days.*[57]

> *In nova fert animus mutatas dicere formas*
> *Corpora; di, coeptis (nam vos mustastis et illas)*
> *Adspirate meis, primaque ab origine mundi*
> *Ad mea perpetuum deducite tempora carmen!*

(*Metamorphoses*, I, 1-4)

The poet anticipates the creation of the world, admitting the existence of the original chaos. He outlines an interesting cosmogony, borrowing philosophical ideas from the Greek thinkers Anaxagoras[58] and Empedocles.[59] The term *semina rerum* – the seeds of things, book 1, verse 9, is also found in Lucretius in his philosophical poem *De Rerum Natura*. The climactic point in the creation of the universe and in the evolution of life on earth was the appearance of man, a creature endowed with reason – *mentis capacius altae*, book I, verse 76, to whom the poet brings an eulogy in the form of an enthusiastic hymn, showing his perpetual aspiration toward the sky:

> *All other animals look downward; Man,*
> *Alone, erect, can raise his face toward Heaven.*[60]

---

[57]Ovid, *Metamorphoses*, translated by Rolfe Humphries, Indiana University Press, Bloomington, 1983, p. 3.

[58]Scriitori greci şi latini…

[59]*Ibidem.*

[60]Ovid, *Metamorphoses*, p. 5.

Pronaque cum spectant animalia cetera terram,
Os homini sublime dedit caelumque videre
Iussit et erectos ad sidera tollere vultus.

(*Metamorphoses*, I, 84-86).

Afterwards, the author of *Metamorphoses* describes the four ages of humanity: the golden age, the silver age, the copper age, and, finally, the iron age. *Aura aetas – The Golden Age*, book I, verse 89, dominated by Saturn,[61] was a time when people lived in complete harmony with nature. This epoch, created by the imagination of man with the mind of a child who believed in fairy tales, is, of course, a fantasy, but the primitive people accepted it as a possible reality, manifesting their nostalgia for the land that gave fruit without having to be worked, and for the country in which rivers of milk and honey used to flow:

Spring was forever, with a west wind blowing
Softly across the flowers no man had planted,
And Earth, unplowed, brought forth rich grain; the field,
Unfallowed, whitened with wheat, and there were rivers
Of milk, and rivers of honey, and golden nectar.[62]

Vet erat aeternum, placidique tepentibus auris
Mulcebant Zephyri natos sine semine flores.
Mox etiam fruges tellus inarata ferebat,
Nec renovatus ager gravidis canebat aristis;
Flumina iam lactis, iam flumina nectaris ibant.

(*Metamorphoses*, I, 107-111)

---

[61] Anca Balaci, *op.cit.*

[62] Ovid, *Metamorphoses*, p. 6.

The paradisiacal picture created by the imagination of the poet for the purpose of conveying the innocence of life on earth is in fact the vision of man at his beginning stage, who comforts his existence by dreaming of impossible states of happiness. Ovid did not share these naive convictions, but reality is not the overriding concern in matters of artistic creation. This peaceful landscape is followed by images of devastating floods. The verses become graver, just like the sky that clouds over and is being crossed by Jupiter,[63] who is throwing terrible thunderbolts toward earth. The description receives powers worthy of the frightful rage of nature, and the deluge devastates everything in its way and drowns all living souls, as well as the little that the poor Romans had:

> *The leaping rivers*
> *Flood over the great plains. Not only orchards*
> *Are swept away, not only grain and cattle, Not only men*
> *and houses, but altars, temples,*
> *And shrines with holy fires.*[64]

> *Expatiata ruunt per apertos flumina campos,*
> *Cumque satis arbusta simul, pecudesque virosque,*
> *Tectaque cumque suis rapiunt penetralia sacris.*

> (*Metamorphoses*, I, 285-287)

---

[63] Anca Balaci, *op. cit.*

[64] Ovid, *Metamorphoses*, pp. 11-12.

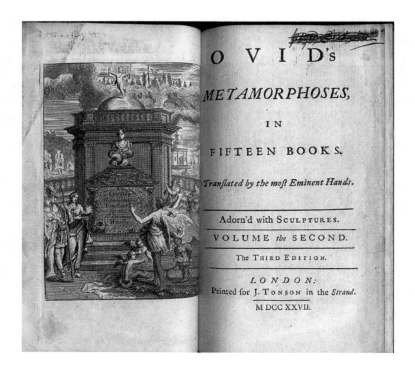

English translation of *Metamorphoses*
published in London in 1727

The description of the deluge is impressive, and the author proves himself a true romantic, who likes to capture in verses the fury of the sky and of unbridled nature.

The frightful aquatic calamity described in book I is followed in book II by the wrath of a ravaging heat wave: Phaëthon, the reckless son of Phoebus,[65] trying to drive the fire horses of the sun, loses hold of them in a moment of absent-mindedness and they run away wildly, reaching close to the earth and burning everything in their way. The fire calamity spreads quickly and is about to burn the entire universe. The poet watches with horror the disastrous spectacle, which he describes with great artistry:

> *The prairies crack, the rivers*
> *Dry up, the meadows are white-hot, the trees,*
> *The leaves, burn to a crisp, the crops are tinder.*
> *I grieve at minor losses. The great cities*
> *Perish, and their great walls; and nations perish*
> *With their people: everything is ashes.*
> *The woods and mountains burn.*[66]

> *Pabula canescunt, cum frondibus uritur arbor,*
> *Materiamque suo praebet seges arida damno.*
> *Parva queror: magnae pereunt cum moenibus urbes.*
> *Cumque suis totas populis incendia gentes*
> *In cinerem vertunt. Silvae cum montibus ardent.*

(*Metamorphoses*, II, 212-216)

If the legend of the deluge might have existed in the memory of the ancient peoples, that of the fire calamity must have been based either on the great droughts or on the volcanic eruptions; the

---

[65] Anca Balaci, *op. cit.*

[66] Ovid, *Metamorphoses*, pp. 34-35.

disastrous fire described by the poet is probably based on a terrible reality.

Afterwards, the transformative legends succeed each other, merging into the ensemble of the work, and the author, amazed, but always attentive to the unfolding of the wondrous mythological comedy, can be spied behind them discreetly, like a true *demiurge*. The heroes, created out of the great collective imagination of the ancient world, let themselves be transformed successively into stones, plants, and animals, just as marble blocks are transformed into faces under the chisel of a great sculptor. Thus, the question arises: if, with the help of a chisel, one can create an everlasting work of art, why would it not be possible to do the same thing with words?

Ovid, like other great poets, created immortal works and succeeded in matching sculptors like Phidias or Praxiteles in his concern for artistic perfection. Thus, Daphne is transformed in a laurel, Io becomes a heifer, Syrinx a reed, Narcissus a flower, Echo an echo, Cygnus a swan, Battus a stone, and Actaeon a stag.[67] The transition from one realm to another is done by respecting the rule of *genus proximus* and no sign of violation appears awkward. An extraordinary example is the description of the transformation of the Maenads into trees, as a punishment for killing Orpheus,[68] the god of music:

> *They looked to see their fingers,*
> *Their toes, their nails, and saw the bark come creeping*
> *Up the smooth legs; they tried to smite their thighs*
> *With grieving hands, and struck on oak; their breasts*

---

[67] Anca Balaci, *op. cit.*

[68] *Ibidem*, see *Menade*.

Were oak, and oak their shoulders, and their arms
You well might call long branches and be truthful.[69]

Dumque ubi sint digiti, dum pes ubi quaerit, et ungues,
Adspicit in teretes lignum succedere suras,
Et conata femur maereni plangere dextra,
Rogora percussit; pectus quoque robora fiunt:
Robora sunt umeri, frondosaque bracchia veros
Esse putes ramos, et non famare putando.

(*Metamorphoses*, XI, 79-84)

The description of the transformation of the Maenads into trees is similar to the Homeric image.

But despite the tragic character of the poem, Ovid does not forget that his own art consists of the use of subtle sensibility. That is why he includes love stories in the poem, giving the work lyrical beauty through the development of deeply human feelings. Thus, Pyramus and Thisbe, Philemon and Baucis, Orpheus and Eurydice, all represent characters who became famous through the intensity of their love, their unlimited devotion, and the power of sacrifice that they demonstrated. The myth of Orpheus[70] occupies an important place in Ovid's *Metamorphoses*. The bard from Rhodope – the one who, through the power of his art, managed to tame even wild beasts – impresses through the tragedy of his pain. He loses his beloved wife, Eurydice, a second time.

The verses that portray the dark realm of the inferno to which Eurydice had returned, because Orpheus did not respect Pluto's condition to not look back, are staggeringly dramatic:

---

[69] Ovid, *Metamorphoses*, p. 261.

[70] Anca Balaci, *op.cit.*

They climbed the upward path, through absolute silence,
Up the steep murk, clouded in pitchy darkness,
They were near the margin, near the upper land,
When he, afraid that she might falter, eager to see her,
Looked back in love, and she was gone, in a moment.
Was it he, or she, reaching out arms and trying
To hold or to be held, and clasping nothing
But empty air?...[71]

Carpitur adclivis per muta silentia trames,
Arduus, obscurus, caligine densus opaca.
Nec procul abfuerunt telluris margine summae:
Hic, ne deficeret, metuens avidusque videndi,
Flexis amans oculos: et protinus illa relapsa est;
Bracchiaque intendes prendique et prendere certans
Nil nisi cedentes infelix adripit auras.

(*Metamorphoses*, X, 53-59)

This moving love story would be repeated throughout the centuries, either through imitations or borrowings, in many artistic works, some of them original creations such as *Orpheus* and *Eurydice* by the German composer Glück.

Toward the end of *Metamorphoses*, in book XV, Ovid describes as an eyewitness the transformation of Caesar into a star. Afterwards, following other poetical examples, he dedicates many verses to Octavian, glorifying him like a god. The homage paid to the emperor must not be confused with a final act of adulation, because the crowning of the poem is not this poetical reverence, but the conviction, proudly declared by the poet, that his work will resist the

---

[71]Ovid, *Metamorphoses*, p. 236.

passage of time and will make his name immortal. Like Horace, Ovid was aware of his talent:

> Now I have done my work. It will endure,
> I trust, beyond Jove's anger, fire and sword,
> Beyond Time's hunger. The day will come, I know,
> So let it come, that day which has no power
> Save over my body, to end my span of life
> Whatever it may be. Still, part of me,
> The better part, immortal, will be borne
> Above the stars; my name will be remembered
> Wherever Roman power rules conquered lands,
> I shall be read, and through all centuries,
> If prophecies of bards are even truthful,
> I shall be living, always.[72]

> Iamque opus exegi, quod nec Jovis ira, nec ignis,
> Nee poterit ferrum, nee edax abolere vetustas.
> Cum volet, illa dies, quae nil nisi corporis huius
> Ius habet, incerti spatium mihi finiat aevi;
> Parte tamen meliore mei super alta perennis
> Astra ferar, nomenque erit indelebile nostrum;
> Quaque patet domitis Romana potentia terris,
> Ore legar populi; perque omnia saecula, fama,
> Si quid habent veri vatum praesagia, vivam.

> (*Metamorphoses*, XV, 871-879)

Metamorphoses assured Ovid a place among the great poets of world literature and contributed to the preservation of many beautiful legends and myths. They would have certainly been lost, like so many other treasures of human genius, had Ovid not had the

---

[72]Ovid, *Metamorphoses*, p. 392.

fortunate inspiration to collect them carefully from Greco-Roman tradition and to use them in his poetry.

The prophecy of the poet came true: his fame as a universal poet preserved his name throughout the centuries. The ending of *Metamorphoses* is grand, without being ostentatious, and it reflects the satisfaction of a worker who has completed his task well.

Along the same lines of serious art, Ovid wrote *Fasti*, an extensive work, which, however, remained unfinished. Its elaboration was begun immediately after the year A.D. 8 and was continued over time, including during part of his exile in Tomis. The poet intended to write it in twelve parts – one for each month of the year – but he only realized six parts before he was exiled. The work was dedicated to Germanicus, although it had initially been dedicated to Augustus.

Fasti consists of a versified calendar and problems of astronomy, like the appearance and disappearance of the constellations:

> *The order of the calendar throughout the Latin year,*
> *its causes, and the starry signs that set beneath the earth*
> *and rise again, of these I'll sing.*[73]

> *Tempora cum causis Latinum digesta per annum*
> *Lapsaque sub terras, ortaque signa callam.*

(Fasti, I,1-2)

The poet evokes the ancient customs, religious ceremonies, chronicles, and annals of the Roman people:

---

[73]Ovid, *Fasti*, translated by James George Frazer, Harvard University Press, second edition, 1989, p. 3.

Here shalt thou read afresh of holy rites unearthed
from annals old,
And learn how every day has earned its own peculiar
mark.[74]

Sacra recognosces annalibus eruta priscis,
Et quo sit merito quaeque notata dies.

(*Fasti*, I, 7-8)

Talking about the month of January, he derives its name from Janus, an old Italic deity, to whom he is praying for the protection of the Roman people. The god, holding a scepter in his right hand and a key in his left, becomes the guide for the poet in deciphering the secrets of the past and in understanding the meaning of certain holidays and traditional customs. The description of New Year's Eve increases the creative energy of the poet and brings him optimism and faith in life:

A happy morning dawns. Fair speech, fair thoughts
I crave! Now must good words be spoken on a good day.[75]

Prospera lux oritur; linguis animisque favete!
Nunc dicenda bona sunt bona verba die.

(*Fasti*, I, 71-72)

He continues by presenting other traditional holidays of the Romans: *Carmentalia, Lupercalia, Feralia, Pariiia, Cerialia, Floralia,* etc.

The third day of the Ides of February, for example, was dedicated to Lupercalia, connected to the cult of Pan, the god of flocks. The poet depicts this ancient tradition, providing

---

[74]*Ibidem.*

[75]*Ibidem*, pp. 8-9.

mythological details, dating back to the proto-history of Rome, when people used to lead very simple lives:

> *Their life was like that of beasts, unprofitably spent;*
> *artless as yet and raw was the common herd.*
> *Leaves did they use for houses, herbs for corn:*
> *Water scooped up in two hollows of the hands to them*
>
> > *was nectar.*
>
> *No bull panted under the weight of the bent ploughshare:*
> *No land was under the dominion of the husbandman.[76]*

> *Vita feris similis nullos agitata per usus;*
> *Artis adhuc expers et rude volgus erat.*
> *Pro domibus frondes norant, pro frugibus herbas,*
> *Nectar erat palmis hausta duabus aqua.*
> *Nullus anhelabat sub adunco vomere taurus,*
> *Nulla sub imperio terra colentis erat.*

> > (*Fasti*, II, 291-296)

Floralia, the holiday of spring, of flowers, was an exuberant celebration that took place between the end of April and the beginning of May. During this festivity, they celebrated the goddess Flora, named Chloris by the Greeks. This time of the year, when people were inclined toward beauty and freshness, is described by the poet in words full of lyricism. It is with great artistry that he describes the delicate flowers, these polychrome ephemera which invite all people who are full of the eternal wish for the regeneration of life to live. The Hours, the Graces participate to the joy of all of nature, spinning with all mankind in a kind of cosmic intoxication, so necessary to man after the winter wakeful state. Again, Ovid's

---

[76]*Ibidem*, p. 79.

sensibility is swirling intensely, like a discharge of suffocating worries, both his own and those of his fellow men:

> Soon as the dewy time is shaken from the leaves,
> And the varied foliage is warmed up by the sunbeams,
> The Hours assemble, clad in dappled weeds,
> And cull my gifts in light baskets.
> Straightway the Graces draw near, and twine garlands
> And wreaths to bind their heavenly hair.[77]

> Roscida cum primum foliis excussa pruina est,
> Et variae radiis intepuere comae,
> Conveniunt pictis incinctae vestibus Horae
> Inque leves calathos munera nostra legunt.
> Protinus accedunt Charites nectuntque coronas
> Sertaque caelestes implicitura comas.

(*Fasti*, V, 215-220)

A poem with an *etiologic* character, influenced by similar writings from the Hellenistic period (*Aitii* by Callimachus),[78] as well as works of Latin tradition (*Origines* by Cato; *De Fastis* by L. Cincius Alimentus),[79] *Fasti* brings a special note in the ensemble of Ovid's work, as well as in all of Latin literature. Although the book includes mythological episodes and, sometimes, even metamorphoses, it is not adjacent with poetry proper and nothing can save it from its dry prosaism, not even the rhetorical style, of which, on other occasions, the author proved himself to be a master. Thus, *Fasti*, without rising above the average level of artistic creation, has a place among proper

---

[77] *Ibidem*, p. 277.

[78] Anca Balaci, *op. cit.*

[79] *Scriitori greci și latini...*, see L. Cincius Alimentus.

writings, and, although today it does not draw the interest anticipated by the ancient author, it is still valuable as a literary document.

CHAPTER III

BANISHMENT FROM ROME

When glory was smiling on him for all eternity – *Metamorphoses* had proved his exquisite talent – and while he was writing the first six books of *Fasti* (during the year A.D. 8 when he was 51 years old), suddenly his life in Rome was ruined: Octavian Augustus, Emperor of Rome, issued a relegation edict which exiled the poet of love and myths to Tomis, a Hellenic city, in the land of the Getae, on the western shore of Pontus Euxinus.

What was the nature of the offence that brought the wrath of the emperor upon the bard? Except for Ovid's writings in exile and a brief mention dated from the fourth century, attributed to Sextus Aurelius Victor,[80] we find no reference by any of Ovid's contemporaries concerning the offence that he committed. Later historians give no indication either, which makes it very difficult, if not impossible, to establish for certain the reasons for Ovid's banishment. Nevertheless, we shall try to establish the causes.

---

[80]*Libellus de vita et moribus imperatorum*, 1, 24.

As we have mentioned, Augustus was determined to improve the morals of imperial Rome, especially of the boisterous nobility, beginning with the eradication of decadent behavior within his own family. Aged and ill, the emperor displayed intolerance for public debauchery, while ignoring what was going on within his own family. Soon, however, the scandalous behavior of his niece, Iulia Minor, became public knowledge and Augustus was distressed. First, he tried to suppress the scandal, resorting to measures that made his family the center of public contempt. Nevertheless, the emperor was undeterred and continued his efforts to put an end to the decline of social morals, this time setting an example by punishing members of his own family. Thus, his libertine niece was exiled, and together with her many others were punished, including Ovid. He was exiled to Tomis (the banishment did not include the confiscation of his wealth) ostensibly for corrupting the youth of Rome through his work, *Ars amandi*. Given the uncertainty surrounding the causes of his banishment, several hypotheses have been formulated, of which three deserve serious attention:

According to the first hypothesis, supported by Bayeux,[81] Cuvillier-Fleury,[82] Boissier,[83] Cartault,[84] Korn-Ehwald,[85] Schanz,[86]

---

[81] A. Bayeux, Preface to the translation of *Fasti*, Rouen, 1788.

[82] A. Cuvillier-Fleury, *Revue de Paris*, 1829, p. 200 ff.

[83] G. Boissier, "L'exile d'Ovide," in *Revue des deux Mondes*, 1867, pp. 580-612 (reproduced in the volume *L'opposition sous les Césars*).

[84] A. Certault, "Encore sur les causes de la relegation d'Ovide," in *Melanges Chatelain*, Paris, 1910, p. 42, ff.

[85] *Metamorphose*, Ehwald-Haupt-Korn, ed., Berlin, 1915-1916.

[86] M. Schanz-K. Hoius-Er. Krüger, *Geschichte der römischen Literatur*, München, 1935.

etc., the main reason for Ovid's banishment was the publication of his collection of erotic poems, *Ars amandi* or *Ars amatoria*.

The second hypothesis, supported by Villeneuve,[87] Nageotte,[88] Plessis,[89] and Rippert,[90] considers Ovid as an accomplice in the plot against Tiberius, the son of Livia, for the purpose of making the nephew of the emperor, Posthumous Agrippa, heir to the throne.

Finally, the third hypothesis, supported by S. Reinach[91] and Jérome Carcopino,[92] is of a mystic-religious nature and maintains that Ovid participated in some mystical, illegal cults and ceremonies, which apparently honored the goddess Isis.[93]

But let us examine what the exiled poet himself confesses in several of his elegies in *Tristia* and *Ex Ponto*. Addressing the emperor, he reproaches him for taking an arbitrary measure and not respecting the penal code:

Thou didst not condemn my deeds through a decree of
                                              the Senate
Nor was my exile ordered by a special court.[94]

---

[87]F. Villeneuve, "Les origins de l'élégie latine," in *Études de littérature latine*, Montpéllier, 1947.

[88]E. Nageotte, *Ovide, sa vie et ses oeuvres*, Dijon, 1872, Paris, 1921.

[89]F. Plessis, *La poésie latine*, Paris, 1909, p. 418.

[90]E. Ripert. *Ovide, pot e de l'amour, des dieux et de l'exil.*

[91]S. Reinach, "L'exil d'Ovide," in *Revue Archéologique*, 1909, p. 145, ff.

[92]Jérome Carcopino. "De la Porta Maggiore la Tomis," in *Orpheus*, I, 1925, pp. 289-313.

[93]Anca Balaci, *Mic dicționar...*, see Isis.

[94]Ovid, *Tristia*, p. 65.

Nec mea decreto damnasti facta senatus,
Nec mea selecto iudice iussa fuga est.

(*Tristia*, II, 131-132)

This raises the question: why did Augustus not bring the accused before a court? Did he circumvent this because his offence was not covered by the letter of the law, or did he seek to prevent a secret of the imperial family from becoming public knowledge? Regardless, in December of the year A.D. 8, he signed a decree ordering Ovid's exile to Tomis.

In the eyes of Roman public opinion, the imperial edict seemed light punishment, as it spared the poet both his wealth and his civil rights. The fact that the judgement seems to have considered public opinion means that the emperor had certain doubts regarding the seriousness of the offence and, although he signed the edict, his hesitating hand must have been guided by another, steadier hand. In any case, we have reason to believe that the banishment of the poet to such a remote place served the interests of the imperial Roman court. Augustus showed his clemency by sparing Ovid's wealth, and the poet was erased from the list of the living without being executed – which would have brought public outrage against the emperor. Thus, the edict, seemingly lenient, constituted a formula that could only have been conceived of by Livia, the stern wife of the emperor. She acted with intelligence and cleverness to pave the way to the throne for her son, Tiberius. The removal of Ovid from Rome seems to have been part of her plan to eliminate successively those who might support another candidate, as well as the pretenders themselves. The decree of banishment had more to do with the removal of an inconvenient witness for the empress rather than with the conviction of an offender. Continuing his attempt to vindicate himself before the law, the poet adds the following:

I lack neither the right nor the name of citizen,
Nor has my fortune been granted to others,
And I am not called "exile" by the terms of thy decree.[95]

Nec mihi ius civis nec mihi nomen abest
Nec mea concessa est aliis fortuna, nec exul
Edicti verbis nominor ipse tui.

(*Tristia*, V, 2, 56-58)

His reasoning in the verses quoted above is only about form but not substance, because he avoids the true cause of his condemnation; even if he escapes the law, he cannot escape the emperor. In *Tristia*, the poet confesses that there were two causes: *carmen* – poetry, almost certainly *Ars amandi*, for the contents of which he was qualified as *doctor obsceni adulterii* – "learned in the shameless adultery"; and the second, a more serious cause: error – a dangerous mistake – which, compared with the noxious *Ars amandi*, represented a much more serious wrong, committed by the poet in a moment of weakness. He refuses, however, to talk about this error.

Carmen, the incriminating poem of his youth, which came into conflict with the imperial measures designed to correct the social behavior of the aristocratic youth, was *Ars amandi* or *Ars amatoria*, a work which modern readers find truly inoffensive. The poet enjoyed being regarded by the youth as a mentor in the mysteries of love, and that was why he gave advice regarding the behavior of men toward women. He praised the silky chestnut hair of Corina – the symbolic embodiment of the adored woman – or he laments the death of her parrot. Could such "trifles, beautifully expressed" threaten the foundations of Augustus's empire?

---

[95]Ovid, *Tristia*, p. 219.

In addition, the collection *Ars amandi* had been written many years before the order for banishment, and no one at the imperial court had previously expressed any objection. However, the truth is that the writings of the mundane poet encouraged the lascivious, unproductive life of the aristocratic youth. It goes without saying that Augustus, Livia, and her son, Tiberius, who in those days controlled the affairs of the empire through their bureaucratic methods and complicated intrigues, could not have given a more drastic warning to libertines than by punishing the one who had sung of their carefree way of life. In this way, poetry contributed to Ovid's banishment to Tomis.

As for the second cause, his *error*, it is presumable that it resulted from the poet's nature and his participation in the orgies practiced by members of Augustus's family. It is possible that he may have been part of the entourage of Iulia Minor, the niece of the emperor, a scandalously libertine woman, who, like her mother, Iulia Maior, who previously had been exiled to the Pandateria Island, was accused of immorality and banished to the Trimerium Island. Although the circumstances are not known, the poet is said to have participated in one of the orgies organized by Iulia Minor, thus seeing her in a compromising situation. He confesses that he saw what he should not have (*Tristia*, II, 1, 100-105).

Some scholars have gone so far as to formulate the hypothesis that "Diana naked" was the Empress Livia herself.

But let us not forget that at the time when these events, which Ovid wrote about in exile, were taking place – at the beginning of the new era – the empress had long passed the age of maturity, which makes less plausible any suspicions regarding her amorous practices.

Therefore, we are probably correct to believe that the term *error* is explained only by an inadvertence in connection to Iulia Minor.

Thus, his main mistake, that of having unintentionally seen, or having contemplated the nude of the imperial niece (in her own house, where Iulia conducted her libertine amorous practices), and, moreover, the fact that it became public knowledge that the poet had committed such a "sacrilege" infuriated Augustus to such an extent that punishment became inevitable. The emperor expected for himself, as well as members of his family, not only full respect, but also religious adoration. This lack of judgement and political tact was probably the great fault of Ovid which resulted in his banishment to Tomis. Livia and her descendants did everything in their power to prevent the poet from ever returning home.

The abstract noun *error* has generated a whole series of suppositions, some of them crossing into the realm of the fantastic. A lot has been and will be written about this *error*, not because it was a common mistake, but because it is also possible to have been of a political nature. It will, however, remain a mystery, sealed by the silence of the one who committed it:

> Though two crimes, a poem and a blunder,
> Have brought me ruin, of my fault in the one I must
> keep silent.[96]

> Perdiderint cum me duo crimina, carmen et error,
> Alterius facti culpa silenda mihi.

> *A poem*
> *&*
> *An Err.*

(*Tristia*, II, 207-208)

Nevertheless, the poet leaves clues for the imagination of the reader to investigate, implying that those responsible for the way Augustus treated him were Livia and Tiberius. Historians of Augustus's reign have explained precisely the role that Livia played in clearing the way to the throne for her son, Tiberius, plotting

---

[96]Ovid, *Tristia*, p. 70.

several assassinations to eliminate other possible candidates. The preference of Octavian Augustus for his nephew, Agrippa Posthumous, was known by Fabia, Ovid's wife, who in her turn had learned this secret from her brother, Fabius Maximus. It is possible that certain indiscretions were made by the poet's slaves, which infuriated Tiberius and Livia. It is possible that the empress asked her husband to eliminate Ovid and punish the emperor's niece, Iulia Minor, who was known to meet with Iulius Silanus at the poet's house. Thus, the poet was accused of pandering – *lenocinium* – by Augustus himself, an unfair accusation that cannot withstand a critical judgement for the obvious reason that Ovid, who had an honorable social status and a good name in the eyes of Roman public opinion, could not have degraded himself through such a dishonorable practice. It is possible, however, that the libertine niece of the emperor might have arranged her meetings with Iulius Silanus without Ovid's knowledge, and one of them might have been witnessed by the host, who, for fear of the terrible consequences, did not bring the incident to the knowledge of Augustus. It is in this sense that we should interpret the following verses:

> *Why did I see anything? Why did I make my eyes guilty?*
> *Why was I so thoughtless as to harbor the knowledge of*
> > *a fault?*
> *Unwilling was Actaeon when he beheld Diana unclothed;*
> *Nonetheless he became the prey of his own hounds.*
> *Clearly, among the gods, even ill-fortune must be*
> > *atoned for,*
> *Nor is mischance an excuse when a deity is wronged.*[97]
>
> *Cur aliquid vidi? cur noxia lumina feci?*
> *Cur imprudenti cognita culpa mihi?*
> *Inscius Actaeon vidit sine veste Dianam;*

---

[97]Ovid, *Tristia*, p. 63.

Praeda fuit canibus minus ille suis.
Scilicet in superis etiam fortuna luenda est,
Nec veniam laeso numine casus habet.

(*Tristia*, II, 103-108).

The poet, in the light of the analogy with Actaeon,[98] witnessed something unusual, probably Iulia Minor nude or her engaging in some type of sexual activity. The legendary hunter spied Diana in a similar situation, and for that she transformed him into a stag, afterwards devoured by his own dogs. Thus, the imperial revenge has a plausible explanation.

The emperor could have undoubtedly forgiven the unintentional indiscretion of Ovid regarding the whims of Iulia, but how could it be forgiven by his vengeful wife, Livia, who was driving away from her husband anyone connected with a direct relative? The sympathy shown by the emperor and also by Iulia Minor for Agrippa Posthumous – at that time in exile on the Planasia Island – for whom certain political circles were trying to pave the way to the imperial succession to the detriment of Tiberius, would constitute a reason for the empress's terrible enmity. Discredited, Iulia and the misfortunate poet could not prevent the ill-fated consequences, both of them suffering the harshness of a severe punishment. The emperor, old and ill, compromised in the eyes of Roman public opinion by the notoriety of his niece's debauchery, let himself be dominated by Livia, designating Tiberius as his successor, against his own wishes. His niece was exiled, and the poet was relegated to a remote corner of Scythia Minor, Tomis, on the shore of Pontus Euxinus.

Therefore, the poet proved himself guilty before Augustus by concealing the immoral act of Iulia, an act condemned by the old

---

[98]Anca Balaci, *Mic dicționar*..., see Actaeon.

Roman morals – *mos maiorum* – but he probably thought that knowledge of the amorous relations between the imperial offspring and Silanus would not have such ill-fated consequences, and, besides, he could not reveal a secret that was not his own and that he had discovered unintentionally. In this situation, revealing what he knew would not have been recommended, especially since the protagonists of the incriminating incident were much more powerful than himself. The silence of the timorous host was compromised by the indiscretion of his slaves:

> *Why tell of the disloyalty of comrades, of the petted slaves*
> *who injured me?[99]*

> *Quid referam comitumque nefas famulosque nocentes?*

(Tristia, IV, 10, 101)

Thus, news of the discovered secret spread throughout Rome, and the poet confesses in his well-known autobiographical elegy:

> *The cause of my ruin, but too well known to all,*
> *Must not be revealed by evidence of mine.[100]*

> *Causa meae cunctis nimium quoque nota ruinae*
> *Indicio non est testificanda meo.*

(Tristia, IV, 10, 99-100)

He no longer tried to vindicate himself, neither did he accuse the emperor of being too harsh. Instead, in verses full of feeling and respect, he asked for his clemency. As we have mentioned earlier, historians, philologists, and literary critics have put forward two other relatively veridical hypotheses.

---

[99]Ovid, *Tristia*, p. 205.

[100]*Ibidem.*

One theory is that Ovid participated in mystical manifestations, intended exclusively for women, in honor of the oriental cult of the Goddess Isis, from which men were prohibited. Another hypothesis is that he attended a meeting of neo-Pythagoreans, in a crypt near Porta Maggiore, in Rome, where the followers secretly celebrated certain mysteries, trying to read the future and the events that would occur in the life of the emperor.

Whatever that *error* might have been, it was discovered while Ovid was visiting his friend Maximus Cotta, on the Island of Elba (*Epistulae ex Ponto*, II, 3). The hesitancy to judge the alleged offender betrays the haste of the imperial house to drive away the poet, who did not even have time to prepare for his sad trip:

> *No time had there been or spirit to prepare what might*
> > *suit best;*
> *My mind had become numb with delay denied me.*
> *I took no thought to select my slaves or a companion*
> *Or the clothing and outfit suited to an exile.*[101]

> *Nec spatium nec mens fuerat satis apta parandi:*
> *Torpuerant longa pectora nostra mora.*
> *Non mihi servorum, comites non cura legendi,*
> *Non aptae profugo vestis opisve fuit.*

> (*Tristia*, I, 3, 7-10)

When he found out that the banishment edict exiled him to Tomis, Ovid was overcome with despair. Fabia, his wife, was shocked; the slaves lamented his departure; his friends deserted him; and the poet, with his sensitive nature, cried with those around him. His grief was great and, unfortunately, he never recovered from it.

---

[101]Ovid, *Tristia*, p. 21.

Overwhelmed by the burden of the terrible sentence, Ovid felt lost. Still, he had the strength to reject Fabia's offer to accompany him into exile, convincing her that it was necessary for her to remain home, to work with their friends to obtain the emperor's pardon. In his elegy "The Night of Exile," the poet passionately describes his parting from his wife:

> *My loving wife was in my arms as I wept,*
> *Herself weeping more bitterly, tears raining constantly*
> *over her innocent cheeks.*[102]

> *Uxor amans flentem flens acrius ipsa tenebat,*
> *Imbre per indignas usque cadente genas.*

(Tristia, I, 3, 17-18)

Unfortunately, most of his friends, admirers, and relatives, deserted him quickly under those sad circumstances and only a few friends came to say goodbye:

> *I addressed for the first time as I was about to depart*
> *my sorrowing friends*
> *Of whom, just now so many, but one or two remained.*[103]

> *Adloquor extremum maestos abiturus amicos,*
> *Qui modo de multis unus et alter erant.*

(Tristia, I, 3, 15-16)

But the edict of Augustus was categorical and the condemned poet, after his return from the island of Elba, could not spend any more time in his home. He had to leave the splendor of Rome and the mild sky of Italy immediately and to start his journey to an unknown place that was troubled by barbarian attacks, a remote land

---

[102] *Ibidem.*

[103] *Ibidem.*

which had recently entered into the Roman Empire, at the time part of the Thracian client-kingdom – *Ripa Thraciae*,[104] or *Scythia Minor*.[105]

He embarked on his journey at Brundisium, just like in his youth when he would leave on a study trip or on a vacation to Greece and the Orient. This time, however, he traveled aboard an old and deteriorated ship which presented few guarantees that it would withstand the tempestuous winter journey; it was a season when few sailers dared to sail across the sea, let alone a frail Mediterranean traveler.

---

[104]*Dicţionar de istorie veche a României*, Editura Ştiintifică şi Enciclopedică, Bucureşti, 1976, see *Ripa Traciae* and *Moesia*.

[105]*Ibidem*, see *Scitia Mica*.

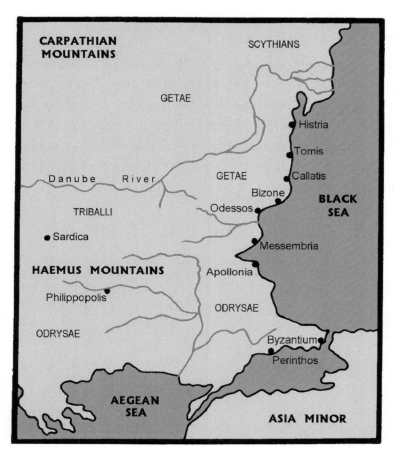

Map showing the western shore of the Black Sea
in the time of Ovid

CHAPTER IV

VOYAGE FROM ROME TO TOMIS

With a broken heart and concerned about facing his inhumane punishment whose somber prospects he could clearly foresee, at dawn on an autumn day Ovid started on his journey to Tomis, his place of exile, never to return.

We do not know exactly what itinerary he followed during the first part of his trip. Historians and his biographers are inclined to believe that he embarked for Greece at Brundisium, which necessarily implies a previous journey on land. Thus, first he would have crossed the mountainous regions of the Italian Peninsula, heading southeast, toward the most important port of the time on the Adriatic Sea, Brundisium, on the shore of Calabria. On his long and tiresome trip, with luggage and slaves – probably accompanied by an escort – the only route Ovid could have taken was through Latium and Campania, with their respective cities, Praeneste and Vanafrum, through the Samnite Mountains guarded by the historic center Beneventum, and from there on to Venusia of Apulia, finally to arrive in the beautiful Adriatic port from where he began the second and most difficult part of his voyage, the one at sea.

Brundisium, despite the sand dunes, brought by the submarine currents, which hinder access to the natural port – the ships anchored a few kilometers away from the shores – had always been the connecting point of Italy with Greece and the Near East. Throughout its history, numerous powerful armies passed through this port, led by aspirants to supreme power who often gained nothing but vain glory. Thus, after Caesar crossed the Rubicon River,[106] the senatorial opposition, headed by Sextus Pompeius, headed for Greece through Brundisium. In 44 B.C., Octavian, at the head of Caesar's troops in Apollonia, started for Italy, landing in Brundisium. But military virtues demonstrated in battle were sometimes followed by true glory protected by the muses that loved the sea.

From this wide-open gate of Italy toward Greece and the Hellenic East, through which inestimable cultural and artistic values passed throughout the centuries, Ovid exited, banished from his own country, one of Rome's great poets, who, through his immortal talent, had brought glory to the one who sent him to die in exile.

---

[106]Between the years 60-49 B.C., Rome's political life was dominated by great personalities, the struggle for supremacy took place between Gaius Julius Caesar and Gnaeius Pompeius (the Great). The two, together with Licinus Crassus, had formed the first triumvirate in the year 59 B.C., but, after a time, Caesar imposed his power. He was also the one who, between the years 58 and 50 B.C., organized the great campaigns for the conquest of Gaul; during his absence, Pompey gained power. Caesar, aware of the danger, returned to Italy. On 10 January 49 B.C., he crossed the Rubicon River, which separated Gaul from Italy, uttering the famous words: *Alea jacta est* – "The die has been cast," and started a civil war. The war lasted until the battle of Pharsalus, in 48 B.C., when Caesar emerged victorious. Pompeius Magnus fled to Egypt where King Ptolemy XII, Cleopatra's brother, killed him.

We do not know how rough and hostile the Ionian Sea was when Ovid traveled toward Achaea.[107] What we do know is that he began writing the first poems of *Tristia* during this sea voyage.

We can easily imagine the thoughts of the unhappy poet when he again saw Odysseus's Ithaca.[108] Helped by the monumental epic poem that has delighted so many generations of admirers of the blind poet from Chios, we can imagine the spiritual comfort that Ovid felt at the sight of the horizons and the landscape that are connected by legend and history to the Homeric city. It must have been with a great deal of sadness that he recalled the verses of Homer's *Iliad*, whose lines were so appropriate for his sad situation:

> The immortals know no care, yet the lot they spin for man is full of sorrow... He for whom Zeus, the lord of thunder, mixes the gifts he sends, will meet now with good and now with evil fortune; but he to whom Zeus sends none but evil gifts will he pointed at by the finger of scorn, the hand of famine will pursue him to the ends of the world, and he will go up and down the face of the earth, respected neither by gods nor men.[109]

But the memory of the wandering Ulysses, and his adventurous journey back to the shore of Ithaca, which he had set out on after the Trojan War, brought Ovid back to the realities of the place. Just then

---

[107]Greece was incorporated in the Roman state immediately after the Third Punic War, in the year 146 B.C., and was transformed into a province with the name of Achaea – after the name of the old Achia in the north of the Peloponnesus.

[108]An island north of Cephallonia, which appears in Homer's poems – Ulysses's home.

[109]Homer, *The Iliad*, translated by Samuel Butler, published for the Classics Club by Walter J. Black, Inc. Rosalyn, N.Y., 1942, book XXIV, p. 385.

he was passing by the shores of the island described in the verses that contain poetical images of an artistry specific to *The Odyssey*:

> I live in Ithaca, where there is a high mountain called Neritum, covered with forests; and not far from it there is a group of islands very near to one another – Dulichium, Same, and the wooded island of Zacynthus. It lies squat on the horizon, all highest up in the sea towards the sunset, while the others lie away from it towards dawn. It is a rugged island, but it breeds brave men, and my eyes know none that they better love to look upon.[110]

The world of *The Odyssey* was left behind with the shore of Ithaca. Once it passed Cephallonia, the ship entered the Gulf of Corinth, deep into Greece. The shores of Aetolia, Phocida, and Beotia to the north, and those of Achaea and Arcadia to the south were all adorned with cities rich in an ancient and tumultuous history, whose beginnings often go back to legends and myths.

Eventually, Ovid arrived at Corinth, the city that guarded the connecting isthmus between continental Greece and Pelopponnesus, on the road that came from Athens and Megara, both of them representing, then as well as centuries later, the great connecting bridge for Greeks everywhere. The poet disembarked in the port of Lechaeum.

Ovid stayed for a while in Corinth, just long enough to be free of the danger of navigating in the middle of winter and at the same time to enjoy once again the delightful city, rebuilt not long before by Caesar himself. There was even a saying about the luxurious and opulent life of this city: *Non licet omnibus adire Corinthum* – "Not everyone has the fortune to go to Corinth."

---

[110]Homer, *The Odyssey*, translated by Samuel Butler, published for the Classics Club by Walter J. Black, Inc. Rosalyn, N.Y., 1944, book IX, p. 104.

But this time the poet was not going to the majestic Hellenic city, whose courtesans protected by Aphrodite would have provided great inspiration three decades earlier. Now he could only allow himself recollections of his long-passed youth when, in Corinth, happy and optimistic, he was admiring edifices and art works, tasting at its fullest a life filled with the refined, intellectual spirit of a commercial city which, already in 146 B.C., had become one of the principal cities of the expansionist Roman Empire.

This rich city, situated at a crossroads, where the "Isthmian Games"[111] had been taking place for centuries – an occasion for Greeks everywhere to gather – gained even more historical glory through its heroic resistance to Rome, as part of the Achaen League.

Many edifices survived the disasters of the year 146 B.C.: Apollo's temple (from the sixth century B.C.); the Pirene Fountain[112] (from the fourth century B.C.), the Acrocorinth, destroyed and rebuilt many times; the archaic Fountain of Glaukes;[113] the great Agora, one of the most famous in Greece, with shops, statues, and beautiful porticos – one of them having seventy-one Doric columns and thirty-four Ionic columns, dating from the fourth century B.C; the theater, where so many famous tragedies had been performed.

---

[111]Every two years, near the city of Corinth, the Pan-Hellenic Games were held. They were similar to the Olympic, Appolonian, and Nemean Games, in which young people from all over Greece, reunited under the patronage of Poseidon, engaged in physical and intellectual contests, competing in gymnastics, music, theater, etc.

[112]One of the curiosities of Corinth in those days. It was said that the Pirene Fountain had been a woman who became a spring because of the tears she shed at her son's death.

[113]A spring under the Acrocorinth; it was captured through several pipes and directed to specially made reservoirs, where there was a splendid portico. Legend has it that is was here that the Nereid Glaukes tried to drown herself to escape the poison of Medea. The well-known Odeon is above the fountain.

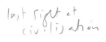

For Ovid, the vestiges of the Corinthian *agora* now appeared as an oasis in the desert of his tortured soul, awaiting its somber future. He enjoyed the delightful, renewed sights.

But the "Corinthian" break came to an end. The wonders he admired, just like in a deceptive dream, would long remain in the poet's memory during his years of his exile.

Conditions favorable for navigation forced him to resume his voyage at sea. He embarked on a new ship, the Minerva, on which he would cross the Aegean Sea. Leaving from the port of Cenchreae, north of Corinth, the ship crossed the Gulf of Saloniki; on the horizon, one could admire the high shore of Attica, dominated by the temple of Hephaestus at Cape Sunion and, advancing south of the island of Euboea, rich in silver, it finally passed out of sight among the giant waves raised by the fury of the unbridled winds. The bitter winds of winter in this part of the world, totally new for the meridional poet, impressed him so much that, with a magical creative force, he described the image of the roaring waters, threatening to swallow him and the entire ship. It appears that it was at that time that the second elegy of *Tristia* took shape, in the form of a ship's log, whose one hundred and ten verses stir powerful emotions – a good reason to consider it a masterpiece of the genre:

> *What mountains of water heave themselves aloft!*
> *Now, now you think, they will touch the highest stars.*
> *What mighty abysses settle beneath us as the flood yawns*
> *apart!*
> *Now, now, you think, they will touch black Tartarus.*
> *Wherever I gaze there is naught but sea and air –*
> *Sea swollen with billows, air athreat with clouds;*
> *And between are the hum and roar of the cruel winds.*
> *The waves of ocean know not what master to obey.*
> *For now Eurus storms mightily from the red east,*

Now Zephyrus comes rushing from the realm of late
                              evening,
now Boreas raves from the dry pole-star,
Now Notus battles with opposing brow.
The helmsman is confused nor can he find what to avoid
Or what to seek; his very skill is numbed by the baffling
                              perils.
We are surely lost, there is no hope of safety,
And as I speak, the waters overwhelm my face.
The billows will crush this life of mine,
And with lips that pray in vain I shall drink
                    the destroying water.[114]

Quantae diducto subsidunt aequore valles!
Iam iam tacturas Tanara nigra putes.
Quocumque aspicio, nihil est, nisi pontus et aër,
Fluctibus hic tumidus, nubibus ille minax.
Inter utrumque fremunt inmani murmure venti.
Nescit, cui domino pareat, unda maris.
Nam modo purpureo vires capit Eurus ab ortu.
Nunc Zephyrus sero vespere missus adest
Nunc sicca gelidus Boreas bacchatur ab Arcto,
Nunc Notus adversa proelia fronte gerit.
Rector in incerto est, nec quid fugiatve petatve
Invenit: ambiguis ars stupet ipsa malis.
Scilicet occidimus, nec spes est ulla salutis,
Dumque loquor, vultus obruit unda meos
Opprimet hanc animam fluctus, frustraque precanti
Ore necaturas accipiemus aquas.

(Tristia, I, 2, 21-36)

---

[114]Ovid, *Tristia*, pp. 13-15.

There is no question that these new circumstances brought about a change in Ovid's style, bringing about a different direction in his artistic creation. What is amazing is his capacity to adapt his talent to totally different circumstances. Moreover, it appears that Ovid's genius thrived on the suffering that began to increase in intensity the closer he came to his destination. Thus, we can conclude that the superficial products of his youth were not the result of a conceptual deficiency, but rather of the circumstances and his nature.

He continued to sail the expanse of the tempestuous sea. But let us allow the poet to describe his own voyage:

I have, and pray that I may always have the protection
*   of golden-haired Minerva*
And my bark draws her name from an emblazoned helmet.
If sails be needed, she runs well at the touch of the lightest
*   breeze,*
Or if oars, the rowers speed her on her way.
She is not content to outstrip in winged course
*   her companion:*
She overhauls the craft that set out no matter how
*   long before;*
Alike she bears the gales and the far-leaping billows;
She is no leaky craft overwhelmed by the raging seas.
Her I knew first at Corinthian Cenchreae
And she remained the faithful guide and comrade of my
*   anxious flight,*
Safe through the power of Pallas amid so many fortunes,
Amid waves roused by the cruel gales.
Now too I pray she may safely cut her path through
*   the gates of the wide Pontus*
And reach the waters of her goal by the Getic shore.[115]

---

[115]Ovid, *Tristia*, p. 49.

Est mihi sitque, precor, flavae tutela Minervae,
Navis et a piela casside nomen habet.
Sive opus est velis, minimam bene currit ad auram,
Sive opus est remo, remige carpet iter.
Nec comites volucri contenta est vincere cursu,
Occupat egressas qaumlibet ante rates,
Et pariter fluctus ferit atque silentia longe
Aequora, nec saevis victa madescit aquis.
Illa, Corillthiacis primum mihi cognita Cenchreis,
Fida manet trepidae duxque comesque fugae
Perque tot eventus etiniquis concita ventis
Aequora Palladio numine, tuta fuit.
Nunc quoque tuta, precor, vasti secet ostia Ponti,
Quasque petit, Getici litoris intret aquas!

(*Tristia*, I, 10, 1-14)

He visited many of the islands scattered throughout the Aegean Sea, whose names have deep roots in the history, myths, and legends of ancient Greece: Lemnos and Imbros – on the latter he spent several days. Finally, he arrived at the famous island of Samothrace, in the north of the sea, and anchored at the port of Zirynthos, where he probably stayed for a while. And he had reason to: that religious center was very famous at the time, because during the Hellenic period it was the seat of the temples dedicated to the Cabiri – the four Oriental gods in whose honor the famous *mistrii* were celebrated: Axieros, Axiersa, Axiersos, and Kasmilos (with the Greek correspondents: Demeter, Persephone, Hades, and Hermes).[116]

How greatly these divinities were worshiped in the Greek cities along the Aegean Sea and the Black Sea, Ovid would realize only when he had reached Tomis, where a *samothrakeion*, a temple

---

[116]*Dicţionar de istorie veche a României*, see Cabiri.

dedicated to the great gods, functioned at that time, as well as later on.

From the northern Aegean island, the route of Ovid's journey changed. The ship Minerva continued to carry his luggage toward Tomis, but the poet preferred to take the overland route through the regions inhabited by the Thracians and then, to the north, by the Geto-Dacians. Ovid chose the land route for two reasons:

First, because he avoided the Black Sea during a season when navigation was almost impossible, both because of the early spring winds, as well as because of the swells caused by the submarine currents.

Second, on land he enjoyed the protection of the authorities of the client kingdom of Thrace and of the military authorities of the province of Macedonia, at that time governed by Sextus Pompeius.[117] Moreover, the poet had the opportunity to see first-hand the regions inhabited by Thracian and Getic tribes, as well as the Hellenic cities along the coast, all the way to Tomis. Let us follow his steps in the same elegiac document from *Tristia*, I, 10, 17-50:

> *I turned my course to the left, away from Hector's city*
> *And came to thy port, land of Imbros,*
> *Whence reaching the Zerynthian shore with a light breeze*
> *My wearied keel touched the Thracian Samos.*
> *From here 'tis but a short leap for one who seeks*
>   *Tempyra on the opposite coast:*
> *Thus far only did my bark attend her master.*
> *For it was my resolve to pick my way all foot through*
>   *the Bistonian land;*
> *She coasted back through the waters of the Hellespont*

---

[117]Protector of the men of letters, who became proconsul of Achaea; he offered Ovid everything he needed for his journey to his place of exile.

Seeking Dardania, bearing the name of its founder,
And thee, Lampascus, secure through the protection of
the country-loving god,
And the strait of that maiden all too insecurely carried
through the narrow waters –
The strait that separates Sestos from Abydos' town –
And Cyzicos clinging to the shores of Propontis,
Cyzicos, the famed work of the Haemonian race,
And Byzantium's shores, that hold the entrance to
the Pontus,
The huge portal to a double sea.
Through all these may she win her way, and driven by
the sturdy breeze
May she have power to pass the shifting Cyaneae,
And the Thynian bay, and after may she hold her course
past Apollo's city
And close beneath the narrow walls of Anchialus.
Thence may she pass the port of Mesembria and Odessos,
And the citadel called after thy name, Bacchus,
And those exiles from Alcathous' walls
Who, so 'tis said, placed on this site their home.
From their land may she come in safety to
the Milesian city
Wither the wrath of an angered god has dispatched me.
If this but happen, a lamb shall fall in sacrifice
to deserving Minerva;
A larger victim ill becomes my poor resources.
Ye too, brother Tyndaridae, whom this isle worships,
Attend in propitious power our twofold way;
For one craft makes ready to pass through the narrow
Symplegadae,
The other to plough Bistonia's waters.

Make ye the winds, though different the places we seek,
Favor the one and no less favor the other![118]

Fleximus in laevum cursus, et ah Hectoris urbe
Venimus ad portus, Imbria terra, tuos.
Inde, levi vento Zerynthia litora nacta,
Threïciam tetigit fessa carina Samon.
Saltus ab hac contra brevis est Tempyra petenti:
Hac dominum tenus est illa secuta suum.
Nam mihi Bistonios placuit pede carpere campos:
Hellespontiacas illa relegit aquas,
Dardaniamque petit, auctoris nomen habentem,
Et te ruricola, Lampsace, tuta deo,
Quodque per angustas vectae male virginis undas
Seston Abydena separat urbe fretum,
Inque Propontiacis haerentem Cyzicon oris,
Cyzicon, Haemoniae nobile gentis opus,
Quaeque tenent Ponti Byzantia litora fauces:
Hic locus est gemini ianua vasta maris.
Haec, precor, evincat, propulsaque fortibus Austris
Transeat instabilis strenua Cyaneas
Thyniacosque sinus, et ab his per Apollinis urbem
Arta sub Anchiali moenia tendat iter.
Inde Messembriacos portus et Odeson et arces
Praetereat dictas nomine, Bacche, tuo,
Et quos Alcathoi memorant e moenibus ortos
Sedibus his profugos constituisse Larem.
A quibus adveniat Miletida sospes ad urbem,
Offensi quo me detulit ira dei.
Haec si contigerint, meritae cadet agna Minervae:
Non facit ad nostras hostia maior opes.
Vos quoque, Tyndaridae, quos haec colit insula, fratres,

---

[118]Ovid, *Tristia*, pp. 49, 51, 53.

Mite, precor, duplici numen adeste viae!
Altera namque parat Symplegadas ire per artas,
Scindere Bistonias altera puppis aquas.
Vos facite ut ventos, loca cum diversa petamus,
Illa suos habeat, nee minus illa suos.

(*Tristia*, I, 10, 18-50)

With the exception of the localities on the micro-Asian shore of Propontida, where the ship cast anchor, along the Thracian shore, beginning from Tempyra, the poet followed much the same itinerary as the ship, meaning that he stopped in the traditional Hellenic cities of Apollonia (Sozopol) and Messembria (Nesseber) in the Thracian territory. Toward the north, in the Getic regions, he went through Odessos (Varna). Today all these cities are in Bulgaria. According to some interpretations, Minerva was waiting for him there and Ovid embarked again. By land or by sea, it is certain that the poet passed through Dionysopolis (Balcic), Bizone (Cavarna), and Callatis (Mangalia). Finally, he arrived in Tomis – today's Constanţa. In the parts of Apollonia and Messembria, he became acquainted with the Thracian tribes of the Odrysii and Nipseeni, and in the north he encountered the Getic tribes of the Crobyzi, Cotensi, and Obulensi. All these tribes were famous for the bravery with which they defended their freedom, threatened by the merciless politics of Rome, which had control over the shore and which was attempting, using diplomatic means rather than force of arms, to integrate their territory, previously under the protection of the client kingdom of the Odrysi Thracians, into the province of Moesia, which was about to be formed.

Presuming that the last part of the journey was also done by sea (because of the improved weather in the spring of the year A.D. 9), the ship Minerva approached the small town of Tomis and the poet, studying the horizons, will have easily distinguished it on the high cliffs that jut out deep into the sea. The ship cast anchor in the gulf, and Ovid had arrived to spend the last eight years of his life amidst a people that he would get to know closely and whose virtues he would glorify through his Latin genius: the Geto-Dacians.

CHAPTER V

THE GETAE AND TOMIS

Who were the Getae who were overwhelming the Greeks in their own city? They were the natives who lived in the Lower Danube region during antiquity. More precisely, they occupied the territory between the Haemus Mountains (the Balkans), the Meridional Carpathians, the southern part of the modern Romanian region of Moldavia, and today's region of Dobrogea, all the way to the shore of the Black Sea. They spoke the same language as their close relatives, the Dacians, who lived in the Carpathian arch of modern Transylvania and Moldavia – territories whose area, analyzed on the basis of archeological evidence, was delimited by much wider ethnic borders. The Geto-Dacians lived within this vast Carpatho-Danubian-Pontic space beginning already in the Bronze Age. They were an advanced civilization, the traces of which have been preserved in settlements and necropolises, today the object of assiduous research. The Thracians, whose tribes lived throughout the entire Balkan Peninsula, except for Greece, along the Dalmatian coast, and north of the Danube, where the Geto-Dacians lived in an area larger than the territory of modern Romania, spoke the same Indo-European language, the differences between tribes being sometimes dialectal or only regional.

Historians and archeologists distinguish between the Southern Thracians, namely those who lived south of the Haemus Mountains, and the Northern Thracians, more precisely those who lived south of the Danube and in today's Wallachian Plain. This classification was done on the basis of certain constant features in their material and spiritual cultures, but also on the basis of certain undeniable literary sources. The border between the Southern Thracians and the Getae, along the Balkan Mountains, is mentioned by Pseudo-Skymnos, v. 738-740: "At the foot of the Haemus Mountains, there is a city called Messembria, which is in the close vicinity of the Getic and Thracian territory,"

The groups of people living between the Lower Danube and the Black Sea, who came into contact with the Greeks earlier, were mentioned in literary sources by the name of Getae beginning in the fourth century B.C. The tribes in Transylvania, the Banat, Moldavia, and the west of the Wallachian Plain are mentioned, in later Latin sources, under the name of Dacians. In reality, the Getae and the Dacians were two tribes of the same blood: they had the same language, the same occupations and beliefs, and their tribal unions, which were formed according to necessities, always acted toward common goals.

Herodotus (*Histories*, IV, 93), Thucydides (*Histories*, II, 96), Strabo (*Geographia*, VII, 3, 10), Polyainos (*Stratagems*, VII, 38), and many other sources mention the Geto-Dacians as participants in events of great historical significance, or as the most important ethnic group in that part of the world between the seventh century B.C. and the second century A.D. The Getae are the ones who daringly confronted the Persian armies of Darius I,[119] between the years 514 and 513 B.C., when the latter had set against the Scythians beyond

---

[119]*Dicționar de istorie veche a României*, see Darius I.

the Mouth of the Danube. Herodotus remarks: "Before reaching the Hister, he defeated the Getae, who believe themselves to be immortal. The Thracians surrendered to Darius without a fight. But the Getae (...) were conquered immediately, even though they are the bravest and most honorable among the Thracians."

They proved their heroism in many other armed conflicts later on, when that *rex Histrianorum*[120] intervened in the dispute between the invading Scythians commanded by Ateas[121] and the armies of King Philip of Macedonia;[122] or when they bravely confronted the impetuous Alexander the Great,[123] in the year 335 B.C., on the Wallachian Plain. Around the year 300 B.C., the leader of a great tribal union, King Dromichaites,[124] defeated Lysimachus, the king of Thrace,[125] and his son, Agathocles. King Zalmodegikos[126] in the region of the Lower Danube had imposed his authority over Histria, the Miselian city on the shore of Lake Sinoe. Also, around the year 200 B.C., Rhemaxos[127] – king on the left bank of the Danube – protected the Greek cities on the sea by virtue of certain agreements, recorded epigraphically. The first Roman attempt, in the years 72-71 B.C., commanded by General M. Terentius Lucullus Varro,[128] to establish Roman domination on the shore of the Black Sea, encountered resistance from the natives, and in the year 61 B.C. the

---

[120] *Istoria Dobrogei*, vol. I, pp. 111 and 129-130.

[121] *Dicționar de istorie veche a României*, see Ateas.

[122] *Ibidem.*

[123] *Ibidem.*

[124] *Ibidem.*

[125] *Ibidem.*

[126] *Ibidem.*

[127] *Ibidem.*

[128] *Ibidem.*

Getic, Bastarn, and Greek forces shamefully defeated the troops of the imprudent Gaius Antonius Hybrida[129] under the walls of the city of Histria.

It was the time when the first centralized and independent Geto-Dacian state was being formed under the leadership of the energetic King Burebista. The occupation of the western shore of the Black Sea, with its Greek city-states, by the Geto-Dacian king led Vasile Pârvan to consider the possibility that the commander of the victorious natives at Histria in the year 61 B.C. might have been the great king himself. It is very likely that it was so if we consider that literary and archeological evidence tells us that Geto-Dacian rule had extended to the Black Sea. The intervention of the ruler of that region in the conflict between Caesar and Pompey, at the battle of Pharsalus in the year 48 B.C., was a consequence of the fact that his state bordered the Roman province of Macedonia on the south.

After the death of Burebista, in 44 B.C., on the territory of Dobrogea – then called Scythia Minor or, between A.D. 15 and 46, Ripa Thraciae – several minor dynasts appeared who fought among themselves and ended up being subjected to Roman rule between the years 29 and 28 B.C.

Those were the protagonists of the historical scene all the western shore of the Black Sea, newly integrated under Roman rule through the victories won by the governor of Macedonia, M. Licinius Crassus,[130] allied with the Geta Roles,[131] against Dapyx[132] and

---

[129] *Ibidem.*

[130] *Ibidem.*

[131] *Ibidem.*

[132] *Ibidem.*

Zyraxes.[133] The Greek city-states on the Black Sea were dominated by the Romans and the interior of the region was under the rule of the Odrysii Thracians – this was the make-up of the foreign force that dominated the Pontic Geto-Dacians, whom Publius Ovidius Naso would soon come to know well:

> *What the people of the land of Tomis are like,*
> *Amid what customs I live, are you interested to know?*
> *Though upon this coast there is a mixture of Greeks*
> $\qquad\qquad\qquad\qquad\qquad\qquad$ *and Getae,*
> *It derives more from the scarce pacified Getae.*
> *Greater hordes of Sarmatae and Getae go and come*
> *Upon their horses along the roads.*[134]

> *Turba Tomitanae quae sit regionis et inter*
> *Quos habitem mores, discere cura tibi est?*
> *Mixta sit haec quamvis inter Graecosque Getasque*
> *A male pacatis plus trahit ora Getis.*
> *Sarmaticae maior Geticaeque frequentia gentis*
> *Per medias in equis itque redique vias.*

(Tristia, V, 7, 9-14)

It is easy to imagine that on the narrow territory between the Lower Danube and the Black Sea, which throughout the centuries had been crossed by numerous invaders, foreign elements remained among the many Getic tribes: Scythians, Sarmatians, Bastarns, etc. We find them mentioned by Ovid, especially the Sarmatians.

The Scythians, whose enclaves had established themselves in the territory around the Lower Danube already at the end of the fourth century B.C., settled especially in the region between Callatis

---

[133]*Ibidem.*

[134]Ovid, *Tristia*, p. 237.

and Odessos. They were the *aroteres* Scythians – the "farming" Scythians – mentioned by Pliny the Elder in his *Natural History*, IV, 11 (18), 41:

> *The entire territory was ruled by the Scythians nicknamed*
> *ploughmen.*

> *Totum eum tractum Scythiae Aroteres cognominati tenuere*

Their leaders minted coins, following the example of the Greeks, at Catallida. Toward the end of the old era and the beginning of the new one, the native Getae almost completely assimilated the Scythians. Only the name of the region – Scythia Minor – remained from them.

The Sarmatians, of Iranian extraction – related, in fact, to the Scythians –, had just arrived in the northern areas of Dobrogea. In the second and first centuries B.C., they gradually penetrated the regions of modern Romania, leaving important traces of their material culture buried beneath the ground. For Ovid, the Sarmatians became, after the Getae, a permanent ethnic presence, and he even learned their language.

> *But now I lie beneath the stars of the Cynosurian Bear*
> *In the grip of the Sarmatian shore, close to the uncivilized*
> *Getae.*[135]

> *Quem nunc suppositum stellis Cynosuridos Ursae*
> *Iuncta tenet crudis Sarmatis ora Getis.*

> (*Tristia*, V, 3, 7-8)

---

[135]Ibid., p. 221.

I myself, I think, have already unlearned my Latin,
For I have learned to speak Getic and Sarmatian.[136]

Ipse mihi videor iam dedidicisse Latine:
Nam didici Getice Sarmaticeque loqui.

(*Tristia*, V, 12, 58-59)

The Getae and Greeks offered the Roman poet exiled in Tomis the understanding and warmth of people who loved and honored him as an illustrious man. He lived among them and they created for him an environment full of solicitude, despite the bitter climate and the places which, according to his repeated confessions, he tolerated with difficulty.

At the beginning of the new era, the fortress-city of Tomis, which would be home to Ovid for more than eight years and would afterwards shelter his remains, was experiencing economic and cultural progress, due to the security enjoyed by its merchants, artisans, and plowmen under the shield of the Roman Eagle.

***

The history of the modern city of Constanța goes back to the time of legends. And the legend is told to us in elegiac distich by Ovid himself, when he explains the origin of the name Tomis. In elegy IX, book III of *Tristia*, the poet, following his inclination for stories inspired from legends, connects the founding of his city of exile to one of the many episodes attributed to the Argonauts and their presumed wanderings across the Black Sea. The heroes on the ship named *Argo* have names with mythical resonances. It is said that many of them fought in the Trojan War. Using the Homeric event, which was confirmed by precious archeological evidence gathered

---

[136]Ibid., p. 255.

by the enthusiastic Heinrich Schliemann,[137] as a reference point, we can easily deduce that the amount of time separating the legends of the Argonauts from the beginnings of Tomis makes any real connection impossible. Nevertheless, let us direct our attention to the imagination set free long ago by the bard, and recall the lyrical and anecdotal part in Ovid's verses for its touching charm: attracted by the richness of Colchis, the country south of the Caucasus Mountains, where the Golden Fleece was found, some daring Greek navigators left to search for it. Fifty of the most venturesome, among whom we mention Hercules, Castor and Pollux, Orpheus, Peleus, Nestor, and Theseus, Argos[138] – the builder of the vessel – embarked on the ship bearing the name of its maker and, having as their leader the ambitious, bold, and always thirsty for glory Jason, the son of King Aeson of Thessaly,[139] left on an adventurous expedition. The legend is that Jason's uncle, Pelias, asked him to bring back the Golden Fleece, with the promise that he would give him the throne.

After many adventures, most of the time accompanied by theft and murder, the Argonauts, without Hercules, arrived at Colchis, where Aeres was king.

---

[137]Heinrich Schliemann (1822-1890), an enthusiastic German amateur archaeologist of an unequaled erudition, who, following the Homeric indications, discovered the ruins of the ancient city of Troy; he also undertook archeological excavations at Mycene, Ordiome, Thirint, and Ithaca, searching for traces of the heroes of *The Iliad* and *The Odyssey*.

[138]See the dictionaries.

[139]A region of Northern Greece, surrounded by Mount Olympus in the north, the Pindus in the west, and the Otharys in the south. The area attracted foreigners at an early time – the first were the Dorians. In the fourth century B.C., Macedonia was conquered and then made part of the Roman and Byzantine empires, and later the Ottoman Empire. Since 1881, it has been part of Modern Greece.

In the beautiful country at the foot of the Caucasus, the Phasus River was flowing, whose waters were rolling, at the same time with sand, grains of gold. It was a practice of ancient times, in those parts, as well as in the land of the Geto-Dacians west of the Black Sea, to lay sheep skins in the river bed, which would capture the grains of gold. That was the Golden Fleece of Colchis searched by the Argonauts – a legendary fiction based on a well-known reality.

At Jason's request, Aetes promised him the precious trophy, but he would give it to him only if his comrades would complete several difficult tasks, trials that were actually impossible to accomplish if the unexpected and the supernatural had not intervened to make possible their realization. Eros,[140] by shooting an arrow in the heart of Aetes's daughter, the beautiful sorceress Medea, made her fall in love with the cunning Jason, whom she helped to accomplish all the tasks given to him by her father. Thus, Jason yoked two wild bulls with steel legs who breathed fire through their noses; he used them to plow a lot where he afterwards sowed dragon teeth, which grew into giants. Following Medea's advice, Jason escaped from the dangerous fantasy creatures by throwing a boulder in their midst, for which they fought each other to the death.

Aetes, suspicious, realized that the daring Argonauts could not have passed his tests without help and he broke his promise, refusing to give them the Golden Fleece. Then, the enamored Medea, consulting with her brother Absyrtus, betrayed her country and helped Jason steal the Golden Fleece. Using her magic, she put the guarding dragon to sleep and the thieves embarked with their precious loot and sailed away. They were accompanied by Medea and Absyrtus, who was taken along by his sister to protect him from their father's wrath. To escape the pursuit of the Colchisians, the

---

[140]Anca Balaci, *Mic dicţionar...*, see Eros.

Argo hurried to the north. With several ships, Aeres made haste to catch them.

Near the mouths of the Hister, when the pursued were about to be caught, the sly Jason used Medea's love again, putting her in another very difficult situation. The beautiful sorceress, blinded by love, did what Jason asked of her: she killed her brother Absyrtus, and afterwards she cut him into pieces, which she threw into the sea. She impaled the head of the unfortunate young man and thrust the stake into the shore, where it could be seen by the Colchisian pursuers.

Indeed, King Aetes recognized his son, stopped, gathered the pieces of Absyrtus's body, and, fearing that his son's soul would otherwise wander through the inferno, he decided to bury him according to tradition. Meanwhile, the *Argo* was now far away.

Aetes returned to Colehis, but he left many of his sailors on the distant shore to guard his son's grave. And because they did not want the terrible deed of Medea ever to be forgotten, the Colchisians built a mound on Absyrtus's grave.

This would be, according to Ovid, the place that gave the name of the Greek settlement *Tomis* or *Tomoi* – with its root in the verb "τεμνω" – "to cut," derived from "τομη–ης" – "cutting."

Ovid used the legend as a pretext to explain in verse the origin of the name of the city where he lived in exile:

> But the ancient name, more ancient than the founding
> of the city,
> Was given to this place, 'tis certain, from the murder
> of Absyrtus.
> For in the ship which was built under the care of warlike
> Minerva –
> The first to speed through the untried seas –

Wicked Medea fleeing her forsaken sire
Brought to a haven her oars, they say, in these waters.[141]

Sed vetus huic nomen, positaque antiquius urbe,
Constat ab Absyrti caede fisse loco.
Nam rate, quae cura pugnacis facta Minervae
Per non temptatas prima cucurrit aquas,
Impia desertum fugiens Medea parentem
Dicitur his remos applicuisse vadis.

(Tristia, III, 9, 5-10)

Ovid tells the reader of the tragedy that might explain the origin of the name of "Tomis," but the unmerciful deed of Medea remains a fiction.

And so at the sight of the approaching sails, she said
'I am caught!' and 'I must delay my father by some trick!'
As she was seeking what to do, turning her countenance
on all things,

She chanced to bend her gaze upon her brother.
When aware of his presence she exclaimed 'The victory
is mine!

His death shall save me!'
Forthwith while he in his ignorance feared no such attack
She pierced his innocent side with the hard sword.
Then she <u>tore him limb from limb,</u>
Scattering the fragments of his body throughout the fields
So that they must be sought in many places.
And to apprise her father she placed upon a lofty rock
The <u>pale hands and gory head.</u>
Thus was the sire delayed by his fresh grief, lingering,

[141]Ovid, *Tristia*, p. 135.

While he gathered those lifeless limbs, on a journey
of sorrow.
So was this place called Tomis because here, they say,
The sister cut to pieces her brother's body.[142]

Ergo ubi prospexit venietia vela 'tenemur,'
Et 'pater est aliqua fraude morandus' ait.
Dum quit agat quaerit, dum versat in omnia vultus,
Ad fratrem casu lumina flexa tulit.
Cuius ut oblata est praesentia, 'vicimus' inquit:
'Hic mihi morte sua causa salutis erit.'
Protinus ignari nee quicquarn tale timentis
Innocuum rigido perforat ense latus,
Atque ita divellit divulsaque membra per agros
Dissipat in multis invenienda Iocis.
Neu pater ignoret, scopula proponit in alto
Pallentesque manus sanguineumque caput,
Ut genitor luctuque novo tardetur et, artus
Dum legit extinctos, triste moretur iter.
Inde Tomis dictus locus hic, quia fertur in illo
Membra soror fratris consecuisse sui.

(*Tristia*, III, 9, 19-34)

To discover the true origins of the city, we must carefully study the documents and archeological evidence. The oldest archeological traces on the territory of today's city of Constanţa date from the Neolithic Age (5500-2200 B.C.) and were discovered near Lake Tăbăcărie:[143] ceramic fragments and tools (silex long blades, scrapers, and slivers) that belong to the Gumelniţa culture – the

---

[142]Ovid, *Tristia*, pp. 135, 137.

[143]A district of Constanţa, with the same name as the neighboring lake, located in the north of the city.

second half of the fourth millennium and the beginning of the third millennium B.C.

The Age of Metals, especially of Bronze, is marked on the territory of the city of Constanţa by a vestige of tools discovered in the year 1966 in the Palas district.[144] It consists of 38 pieces (axes, sickles, a knife point, and bronze plates). Their technical characteristics show intra-Carpathian and extra-Carpathian influences, as well as some analogies with the northwestern Caucasus region. A special interest is presented by the plates, a local alloy used for new tools. The vestige dates from approximately 1300 B.C., therefore from the period of transition to the Iron Age, when the primitive commune disintegrated and there appeared the inherent social differentiations generated by the new developments.

Nevertheless, the civilization on the western shore of the Black Sea cannot be revealed solely on the basis of archeological and written sources, the latter making references to events that took place as far back as the seventh century B.C.

The data on the first part of the Iron Age, Hallstatt (1200-450 B.C.),[145] and the second, La Tène (450 B.C.-the first century A.D.)[146] is considerable. We also have information about the population that lived in this region: the Geto-Dacians. They were the ones who received the visitors from Hellas who came in search of new possibilities.

At the end of the seventh century B.C., as part of the great process of Greek colonization on the Black Sea coast, the city of

---

[144]Another district of Constanţa, in the southwest.

[145]The name of the first part of the Iron Age, named after the German village where remains were first found.

[146]The name of the second part of the Iron Age, which in Dobrogea lasted from the year 450 B.C. until the first century A.D.

Histria was founded, on the shore of today's Lake Sinoe. In the sixth century B.C., Tomis, modern Constanța, was attested to, as was Callatis, modern Mangalia.

Archeological investigations on the territory of Constanța, and analogies with Histria and Callatis, increase the possibilities for learning about the most distant past of the city. The best spot for systematic research has been the courtyard of the cathedral, toward the south-southeastern edge of the promontory. Here, the land was spared from modern diggings, with the exception of the surface stratum, scraped some time ago, which contained vestiges from the fourth to the seventh century A.D. Deep into the ground, twelve strata have been identified with characteristic traces of material culture, covering the period between the sixth century B.C. and the sixth century A.D. The deepest strata that reveal a Greek civilization, mixed with a Geto-Dacian one, contains Histrian coins of the type "with a wheel," which had four spokes all one side and the inscriptions IST-ISTROS, Histria, the place where they were issued (in the fifth century B.C.). Even more important is the discovery of vestiges from the sixth century B.C. The diggings uncovered the outlines of some cottages with the floor deep into the ground, some of them revealing traces of burns, maybe the result of a fire caused by the Persian invasion between 514-513 B.C. Such archaic elements are also found at Tariverde[147] and Histria. In these cottages lived both Geto-Dacians and Greeks. We cannot exclude the possibility that the Hellenic city was built upon a native settlement. Whole ceramic vessels as well as fragments, dating from the sixth century B.C., were

---

[147]Tariverde, a Getic settlement, was strongly influenced by the Greek civilization in Histria, which was situated very close to it. It existed for a long period of time, until the Roman period. It appears to have been an important economic and agricultural center for Histria, the city of Lake Sinoe.

found in these cottages: Chios amphorae[148] (some with inscriptions painted with red dye); micro-Asian Greek bowls and cups; Clazomenian[149] and Corinthian[150] ceramics; a whole Ionian crown vessel;[151] a Chios *olpai*;[152] among the rest of the pieces, there were large quantities of native, Geto-Dacian ceramics, made from a porous, dark brown, impure paste.

Also from the sixth century date the twenty-four arrow tips with three edges (of the Scythian type) and another thirty leaf-shaped points, without a tip and with a peduncle. They are the well-known pre-monetary symbols[153] that served, in the ancient period, as a commercial standard before the appearance of the coin proper.

Therefore, proof of the existence of Tomis dates from the sixth century B.C. Undoubtedly, it had this name. Coins have been found, issued later in its mints, bearing the symbolic face of its legendary founder, Tomos. Nevertheless, a few specifications must be made. Although the city was founded in the middle of the sixth century

---

[148]The Chios amphorae are some of the oldest types of imported vessels – from the Island of Chios in the Aegean Sea. They are dated between the sixth and fourth centuries B.C.

[149]Fine ceramic painted in red, with geometric and vegetal motifs, dating from the sixth century B.C., produced in workshops in Clazomenai in Greece.

[150]Small vessels, but very fine, imported from Corinth, in the sixth century B.C.

[151]A small vessel, with a very special form, rounded, with a narrow neck placed laterally and a handle that covers the top part of the receptacle. It was meant to preserve ointments and perfumes and dates from the sixth and fifth century B.C.

[152]A very small and simple receptacle, designed for the preservation of ointments, dating from the sixth and fifth century B.C.

[153]In the sixth century B.C., in view of the development of commercial exchanges among the Pontic Greek cities and the native population, before the appearance of the coin proper, symbols of exchange were created in the shape of blunt arrow points. They were cast in bronze, in numerous molds and series.

B.C., its name is first mentioned in literary sources with reference to an event that took place in the third century B.C. (cf. Memnon, *Fragmenta historicorum Graecorum*, III, B, 21, pp. 347-348), during the war between the Histrian-Callatian coalition and Byzantium. During the Greek period and later, in the Roman period, the documents use the names *Tomeos, Tomoi, Tomoe, Tomeis*, etc., but the most frequently used forms were *Tomis* and *Tomi*.[154]

The etymology of the toponym has been interpreted as being either of Greek origin or of Thracian (Geto-Dacian) origin. According to the first hypothesis, the toponym is a variant of a number of Hellenic words, whose meaning refers to the seemingly carved shape of the high promontory on which Tomis stands.

The second hypothesis, with which most scholars agree, is that the toponym has a Geto-Dacian origin, having derived from the Thracian words *tomarus, tumulos*, etc., which designate the notion of "elevation." According to this theory, the name refers to the distinctive form of the promontory inhabited by the Geto-Dacians much earlier than the arrival of the Greeks in the sixth century B.C., who continued using the name given to the place by the inhabitants. This hypothesis is verified by recent archeological diggings that reveal not only the cohabitation of the Greeks with the natives, but also the latter's dominance on the peninsula.

The literary sources and the inscriptions in stone or on coins use this name to refer to the city until late in the first decades of the seventh century A.D. In parallel, however, next to the name *Tomis* or *Tomi*, we find another toponym dating from the sixth century A.D., that of *Constantiana* (Hierocles, *Synecodemos*, 637, 6; Procopius from Caesarea, *De aedificiis*, 307, 51). This led some

---

[154]Radu Vulpe, *Histoire ancienne de la Dobroudja*, Bucureşti, 1938, p. 62 and nt. 1; Iorga Stoian, *Tomitana*, Bucureşti, 1962, pp. 13 ff.

historians to seek explanations that stray from the factual evidence. Some of them argue that there were two different cities, while others believe that Tomis and Constantiana were one and the same – which is likely, since, already prior to the seventh century A.D., the form *Constanţa*, with its variants, has been exclusive.

In the tenth century A.D., Constantine Porphyrogenetos (*De admin-istrando imperio*, 9, 96-99) recorded, among other cities on the shore of the Black Sea, the city of *Constanţa*.

Historians explain the name in the form *Constantiana* or *Constantia* through the building, in the fourth century A.D., during the Constantinian dynasty,[155] of a fort neighboring Tomis, which had this name attributed to it by a member of the dynastic family; in the following centuries, the name imposed itself onto the entire city.

The Turks would call it *Küstendje*, an adaptation in their own language of the above-mentioned Latin (Byzantine) form. Beginning in the year 1878, after the reintegration of Dobrogea within the natural borders of Romania, the Romanians renamed the city *Constanţa*, the name that they and the Genoese had used for it in the Middle Ages.

The findings of archeologists lead to the conclusion that Tomis developed at a slower pace than Histria and Callatis during the fifth and the fourth centuries B.C. For a long time, it was an emporium or, in the constitutional-juridical concept of the Greeks, a polis – city-state – with its own laws and leadership rules, identical to those of the colonists who arrived from the metropolis of Milet. They had left

---

[155]Constantine the Great (A.D. 306-337) was the first emperor of a dynasty with several emperors with similar names, which dominated the Roman Empire during the fourth century A.D.; the imperial seat was in Constantinople – the former Byzantion –, a city on the coast of Propontida, which in the year A.D. 330 took the name of its founder.

their lands trying to escape Persian oppression and searching for new opportunities. In the southwest of the promontory of Pontus Euxinus, the gulf, surrounded by a high shore, was hospitable to them, allowing them a long and peaceful cohabitation with the native Geto-Dacian population.

Despite its position, favored by the gulf and the vicinity of the valley of Carasu,[156] which united it with the Danube, the economy of Tomis in its first centuries of existence felt the effects of the commercial dominance established by Histria in the area of the Danube Delta, as well as the intense commerce in grain that gave Callatis a preeminent position in earlier times.

We have no written information from the fifth and the fourth centuries B.C. This is compensated for, however, by the numerous remnants of material culture discovered all over the territory of the city. The necropolis of the epoch, investigated as a result of recent construction in the area of the old train station, revealed Attic vessels with black oil varnish, others with black and red paintings, statuettes of a Tanagra type, gold and silver jewelry, coins, objects for everyday use, etc. The archeological discoveries, both the accidental ones as well as those resulting from the excavations at the cathedral, provide valuable information about this period. Besides the coins "with a wheel" issued at the mints in Histria, they revealed stone and earth walls dating from the fifth century B.C. and stone pavements from the same period. Geto-Dacian and imported Greek ceramics from the fourth and third centuries B.C. are extremely abundant. Important numbers of amphorae of the Thassos, Heraclea, Sinope,

---

[156]A depression that divides the Dobrogean plateau in two, from west to east. In distant geological eras, it could have been an arm of the Danube. It is extremely fertile and, throughout history, numerous settlements were established there which are now the objects of important archaeological research.

Rhodes types have been discovered, many of them with stamps on the neck or the handle, with the name of the magistrates or the priest of the city of origin, or with the trademark of the workshop. All the amphorae served commercial purposes, namely the transportation of oil, wine, and honey. As early as that time, the Greek merchants in Tomis had a well-organized commercial network. The products that they purchased from the Geto-Dacians – grain, animals, honey, cheese, fish, slaves, etc. – travelled by sea to the most remote cities on the coast of the Black Sea or the Mediterranean Sea. In exchange for them, they would bring back artifacts and vegetal goods: weapons, tools, jewelry, clothing, superior wine, olive oil, resins, etc.

There is no information about social or administrative life in the city, but we can reconstruct this by analogy with Histria, where, at the end of the fifth century and the beginning of the fourth century B.C., the oligarchic regime was overthrown, making room for a new democratic order based on slavery. Legislative and executive institutions appeared, including magistrates and civil servants. The popular assembly and the council of elders were the consultative bodies; the archons were magistrates who dealt with administrative issues, the hegemons dealt with military issues, the *agoranoms* were the supervisors of the agorae and the port – these are only a few examples. The citizens were divided, according to tradition, into so-called tribes, which, as in the case of other Miletian cities, were *Argadeis, Aigikoreis, Boreis, Gelontes, Hopletes*, and *Oinopes*. Much later, in the Roman period, the Roman tribe joined them.[157]

We do not have specific information about the way the city of Tomis, with its defense walls, confronted the Scythian danger in the fourth century B.C., the Macedonian attack led by Philip II in the year 339 B.C., or the attack of General Zopyrion in the year 326

---

[157] *Dicționar de istorie veche a României.*

B.C.[158] What is certain is that the west-Pontic Greek cities suffered under the oppression of Lysimachus of Thrace, whose abuses drove them to revolt. For a long time, the citizens of Callatis led the rebels (313-306 B.C.), who were joined by the Geto-Dacian natives, but their uprising ended in defeat.

Shortly after, favorable conditions allowed Tomis to come out of its anonymity. The sanding of the port of Histria led to the gradual stagnation of its commerce on the Danube and enabled Tomis, which was connected to the Danube through what is now the valley of Carasu, where, in the third century B.C., the city of Axiopolis appeared.[159] The latter served very well as a storage place for the goods accumulated from the riverside areas of the Danube later to be sent east, to Tomis.

But, as an emporium, Tomis encountered many vicissitudes. Even if, as is believed, it did not suffer from the invasion of the Celts in 280 B.C., it was affected by the war between Callatis, allied with Histria, and Byzantium.

In the year 260 B.C. a war took place of which we learn about from a written document of the time, namely that of Memnon: "... a war broke out, started by Byzantium against Callatis, which was a colony of Heracleans, and also against Histria, for the emporium of Tomis, which was a neighbor of Callatis. The latter intended to create there its own monopoly..." Therefore, the Histria-Callatis coalition fought with Byzantium, which was allied with Tomis. Byzantium was victorious, but Tomis escaped the control of the victor, and the

---

[158]*Ibidem*, see Zopyrion.

[159]The ancient city of Axiopolis, founded probably at the end of the fourth century or the beginning of the third century B.C., underwent a considerable evolution during the Roman period. Today, it is the city of Cernavodă, at the end of the bridge built by Anghel Saligny in 1895.

road to progress was open to it, in conditions of autonomy. This is confirmed by the fact that, beginning in 250 B.C., the city of Tomis issued its own coins for the first time. Constructions of considerable proportions appeared: public and private edifices, temples, paved streets; the port was expanded and its activity increased; a large agricultural territory was established.

Conflicts with the Geto-Dacian natives or with the Bastarns and the Scythians during the second century B.C. created great difficulties for the inhabitants of the city, who defended themselves not as much by force of arms as through their excellent diplomatic skills. A civic guard was created to keep watch along the defensive walls of the city for repeated attacks by enemies. But along with these common events, in the first century B.C. others occurred that would change the historical course of the city, as well as of the entire region between the Lower Danube and the Black Sea, called Scythia Minor.

Rome extended its control over almost the entire Balkan Peninsula, all the way to the Haemus Mountains. The Thracian state, between the Rhodope and the Haemus Mountains, became a client state. The efforts of Mithridates VI Eupator, the king of Pontus,[160] to resist by force of arms between the years 74 and 73 B.C. failed for a third time. Immediately afterwards, between 72 and 71 B.C., the west-Pontic cities, allies of the courageous king, were occupied by the Romans, who signed "treaties of alliance" with them, which in reality were a subtle means to win their trust. But the abuses that followed drove both the Greeks and the natives to a great revolt in 62-61 B.C. The armies sent to repress the rebellion were defeated below the walls of the city of Histria. It appears that the author of this victory was Burebista since, a few years afterwards, the Geto-

---

[160] *Dicţionar de istorie*, see Mithridates VI.

Dacians dominated all of the Greek cities at the Pontus Euxinus, from Olbia in the north all the way to Apollonia (Sozopol) in the south.

Roman expansion at the mouth of the Danube, which meant first establishing control over the coast, represented an older goal of the Senate. Only under Augustus, did the legions of M. Licinius Crassus, at that time governor of Macedonia, succeed in subjecting the rivaling local dynasts to Roman rule. Once concluded, the Roman conquest lasted for over seven centuries. First the coast and later the entire region of modern Dobrogea became an integral part of one of the greatest empires of antiquity.

Thus, a new and flourishing epoch began for Scythia Minor. The main beneficiary was Tomis, which was offered a preeminent economic position during the Roman period, its citizens adapting to the new conditions. This was the climate in Tomis when Ovid arrived. As the authority of Rome was not yet consolidated, the poet describes the precarious aspects of the epoch inaugurated by the Romans, the Geto-Dacians being the ones who constantly made fierce attacks to regain possession of their traditional territories, now under the control of Odrysian garrisons, faithful to Rome.

> *For when the guard from the lookout has given the signal*
> *of a raid,*
> *Forthwith I don my armour with shaking hands.*
> *The foe with his bows and with arrows dipped in poison*
> *Fiercely circles the walls upon his panting steed;[161]*
>
> *Naill dedit e specula custos ubi signa tumultus,*
> *Induimus trepida protinus arma manu.*

---

[161]Ovid, *Tristia*, pp. 163, 165.

Hostis, habens arcus imbutaque tela venenis,
Saevus anhelanti moenia lustrat equo;

(*Tristia*, IV, 1, 75-79)

Augustus chose Tomis as the place for Ovid's exile as a result of the recent integration of the west-Pontic shore into his empire. The coast was guarded by a fleet and had a military and administrative institution, especially created, called *Praefectura Orae Maritimae*, headed by a commander of the *Praefectura* of the shore. In the first years of its existence, it was under the control of the proconsul of the province of Macedonia, but after the creation of Moesia in the year A.D. 15, it was subordinated to its proconsul. We find echoes of the precarious situation of the new regime in the elegies that Ovid wrote in Tomis.

[The Ciziges, the Colchi, the hordes of Teretei, and
the Getae
Are scarce fended off by the interposition of the Danube's
waters.]
Though others have been exiled for weightier cause,
A more remote land has been assigned to no one;
Nothing is farther away than this land except the cold
and the enemy
And the sea whose waters congeal with the frost.
Here is the end of Rome's domain on the ill-omened
Euxine's shore;
Hard by the Basternae and Sauromatae hold sway.
This land comes last of all beneath Ausonian law,
Clinging with difficulty to the very edge of thy empire.[162]

[Ciziges et Colchi Tereteaque turba Getaeque
Danuvii mediis vix prohibentur aquis;]

---

[162]Ovid, *Tristia*, pp. 69, 71.

Cumque alii causa tibi sim graviore fugati,
Ulterior nulli, quam mihi, terra data est.
Longius hac nihil est, nisi tantum frigus et hostes,
Et maris adstricto quae coit unda gelu.
Hactenus Euxini pars est Romana sinistri:
Proxima Bastarnae Sauromataeque tenent.
Haec est Ausonio sub iure novissima, vixque
Haeret in imperii margine terra tui.

(*Tristia*, II, 191-200)

The repeated and violent attacks of the Getae left of the Danube against some cities on the Dobrogean shore, a natural consequence of their awareness that the land they lost to the Romans and the Odrysii belonged to them and had to be recovered by force of arms, are confirmed by the events at Aegisos in A.D. 12 and in Troesmis[163] in A.D. 15.

We learn of a first attempt by the Getae to conquer Aegisos in *Epistulae ex Ponto*:

An old city lies hard by the bank of Hister of the double
                                                      name,
Scarce accessible because of its walls and the site.
Aegisos, the Caspian, if we may believe the native tale,
Founded it and gave it his own name.
The wild Getae took it after they had destroyed the
                           Odrysii in a warfare of surprise,
And raised their arms against their king.
He, mindful of the mighty race which his own valor
                                                 enhances,
At once approached with a following of countless
                                                 warriors.

---

[163] *Ibidem.*

Nor did he depart until with deserved slaughter of
                                        the guilty

[He beat down the presumptuous spirit of the people.][164]

Stat vetus urbs, ripae vicina binominis Histri,
Moenibus et positu vix adeunda Ioci.
Caspios Aegisos, de se di credimus ipsis,
Condidit, et proprio nomine dixit opus.
Hanc ferus Odrysiis inopino Marte peremptis,
Cepit et in regem sustulit arma Getes.
Ille memor magni genesis, virtute quod auget,
Protinus innumero milite cinctus adest.
Nec prius abscessit, merita quam caede nocentum
[Audaces animos contuderat populi].

(*Epistulae ex Ponto*, I, 8, 11-20)

The man most praised by the poet for the way he fought in the battle against the Getae at Aegisos is the primipilar centurion Vestalis, one of the first commanders of the praefectura of Tomis, who came to the aid of the Odrysii detachments at the Danubian border.

The second episode, connected also to a well-known Geto-Dacian toponym, Troesmis, is narrated in *Epistulae ex Ponto*:

The commander of this region, Graecinus, was till
                                        recently Flaccus,
Under whose charge the turbulent banks of the Hister
                                        were safe.

He held the Moesian tribes to loyal peace,
He cowed with his sword the Getae who trust in the bow.

---

[164]Ovid, *Tristia/Ex Ponto*, translated by Arthur Leslie Wheeler, second edition, revised by G.P. Gould, Harvard University Press, first published 1924, reprinted with corrections 1996, pp. 305, 307.

He recovered with swift valour captured Troesmis,
Dyeing the Danube with barbarian blood.[165]

Praefuit his, Graecine, Iocis modo Flaccus et illo
Ripa ferox Histri sub duce tuta fuit.
Hic tenuit Moesas gentes in pace fideli,
Hic arcu fisos terruit ense Getas.
Hic raptam Troesmin celeri virtute recepit,
Infecitque fero sanguine Danubium.

(*Epistulae ex Ponto*, IV, 9, 75-60)

These verses are part of a letter sent to Rome in the year A.D.
16 to Consul Pomponius Graecinus,[166] whose brother, L. Pomponius
Flaccus[167] (whose name is tied to the victory won at Troesmis by the
Roman and Odrysiian armies), would become governor of Moesia in
A.D. 18.

But these are historical reflections that belong to the later work
of the exiled poet.

***

It is now necessary to look at the entire literary work of Ovid
dating from his exile in Tomis and to give the reader the opportunity
to understand the creations of the poet whom Romanians today
rightfully consider to be the first bard of their land by the sea.

---

[165] *Ibidem*, pp. 459, 461.

[166] A capable military commander, who was also a very cultured man, a lover
of art and literature. Ovid often appealed to him for his services, as he was an
influential personality.

[167] The brother of Pomponius Graecinus. In A.D. 18, he became governor of
Moesia. Before that, in A.D. 15, he recovered Troesmis from the Getae who
were claiming the territories on the right bank of the Danube that they had lost
to the Odrysii Thracians, the allies of the Romans.

When fate drove him away from the sweet atmosphere of imperial Rome and sent him to a place that seemed to give birth to the boreal frost, "the one that killed the flowers," poetry was the only comfort that the unfortunate poet had. Like all those persecuted, Ovid laments, exaggerates his pain, and distorts his impressions, whether on purpose or not, yet he does not allow himself to be overcome. He only exchanges the cheerful, light tonality of his poetry with a melancholic one. Between the years A.D. 8 and 17, he wrote two famous collections of elegies, *Tristia* and *Epistulae ex Ponto*, true masterpieces of ancient literature. These elegies of unequaled artistic value kept alive, for two thousand years, interest in their content, unique in world literature in general and in Romanian literature in particular.

Tristia, a collection made up of five books, was written between the years A.D. 8 and 12. The component parts are mostly elegies and are characterized by sincerity, emotional force, and pathos, the latter being meant to stir the compassion of those he addressed. As in the largest part of his work, Ovid uses the mythological fund as an element of comparison for current events and his style often becomes rhetorical, this time out of need to ease his sufferings. Thus, if his elegiac discourses are not written in a form most appropriate to the poetic canons, they put us in a situation to receive directly their emotional charges.

Elegy I of book I, written during his voyage to his place of exile, is a kind of introduction to his work, an accompanying word to the letter he sent to Rome, in a simple style, without any literary ornaments:

Little book, you will go without me – and I grudge it not –
To the city, whither alas your master is not allowed to go!
Go, but go unadorned, as becomes the book of an exile;

In your misfortune wear the garb that befits these days
of mine.[168]

Parve – nee invideo – sine me, liber, ibis in urbem,
Ei mihi, quo domino non licet ire tuo!
Vade, sed incultus, qualem decet exulis esse;
Infelix habitum temporis huius habe.

(*Tristia*, I, 1, 1-4)

This first poetical missive that Ovid sent to Rome shows his ardent need to communicate with the ones he left behind, so far away. Even in this epistolary composition he is exigent with himself, discussing the conditions in which art is created, requiring peace and serenity.

Poetry comes fine spun from a soul at peace;
My mind is clouded with unexpected woes.
Poetry requires the writer to be in privacy and ease;
I am harassed by the sea, by gales, by wintry storms.
Poetry is injured by any fear; I in my ruin am ever
*   and ever*
Expecting a sword to pierce my throat.[169]

Carmina proveniunt animo deducta sereno;
Nubila sunt subitis pectora nostra malis.
Carmina secessum scribentis et otia quaerunt;
Me mare, me venti, me fera iactat hiems.
Carminibus metus omnis obest; ego perditus ensem
Haesurum iugulo iam puto iamque meo.

(*Tristia*, I, 1, 39-44)

---

[168]Ovid, *Tristia*, p. 3.

[169]*Ibidem*, p. 5.

The main themes of *Tristia* are the adventures of the poet's voyage at sea and his memories about Rome and his birth place. He describes with an exquisite pictorial force the images of the turmoil at sea, the assault of the breakers with foaming manes and abysmal depths, the elements of blind nature, the winter wind, and the terror of those on the fragile ship. The image reminds one of the description of the storm at sea in the second book of *The Aeneid*. Therefore, it is in *Metamorphoses* and *Tristia* that we must search for Ovid as a poet, and not in the mundane opuscule *De medicamine faciei*. But let us pause for a moment in front of this terrible spectacle of the unbridled sea:

> *Wretched me! what vast mountains of water heave*
> *themselves aloft!*
> *Now, now you think they will touch the highest stars.*
> *What mighty abysses settle beneath us as the flood yawns*
> *apart!*
> *Now, now you think they will touch black Tartarus.*
> *Wherever I gaze there is naught but sea and air –*
> *Sea swollen with billows, air athreat with clouds;*
> *And between are the hum and roar of the cruel winds.*
> *The waves of ocean know not what master to obey.[170]*

> *Me miserum, quanti montes volvuntur aquarum!*
> *Iam iam tacturos sidera summa putes.*
> *Quantae diducto sunsidunt aequore valles!*
> *Iam iam tacturas Tartara nigra putes.*
> *Quocumque aspicio, nihil est, nisi pontus et aër,*
> *Fluctibus hic tumidus, nubibus ille minax.*

---

[170] *Ibidem*, pp. 13, 15.

Inter utrumque fremunt inmani murmure venti.
Nescit, cui domino pareat, unda maris.

(*Tristia*, I, 2, 19-26)

Later on, in elegy 12, book III, he thinks again of his dear Sulmo and of Rome from which he was banished, talking about them with pure affection and surrounding them in light .and vegetal exuberance. This elegy proves Ovid's vocation for singing of serene beauty, as well as his sensitivity and love for his country:

Now merry boys and girls are plucking the violets
That spring up unsown in the fields,
The meadows are abloom with many-coloured flowers,
The chatty birds from unschooled throats utter a song
                                                    of spring,
And the swallow, to put off the name of evil mother,
Builds beneath the rafters the tiny house that cradles
                                                    her young.
The grain that lye in hiding beneath the furrows sends
                                                    forth
From the unfrozen soil its tender tips.[171]

Iam volam puerique legum hilaresque puellae,
Rustica quae nullo nata serente venit;
Prataque pubescunt variorum flore colorum,
Indocilique loquax gutture vernat avis;
Utque malae matris crimen deponat hirundo
Sub trabibus cunas tectaque parva facit;
Herbaque, quae latuit Cerealibus obruta sulcis,
Exerit e tepida molle cacumen humo;

(*Tristia*, III, 12, 5-12)

---

[171]*Ibidem*, p. 147.

But through an association of ideas, the beauties of the country remind him of the drama of the last night he spent in Rome. Overwhelmed by the pain caused by the separation from his family, Ovid would never forget that nightmarish night that would haunt him until the end of his life.

> *When steals upon me the gloomy memory of that night*
> *Which marked my latest hours in the city –*
> *When I recall that night on which I left so many things*
> > *dear to me,*
>
> *Even now from my eyes the teardrops fall.*[172]

> *Cum subit illius tristissima noctis imago*
> *Quod mihi supremum tempus in urbe fuit,*
> *Cum repeto noctem, qua tot mihi cara reliqui,*
> *Labitur ex oculis nunc quoque gutta meis.*

> (*Tristia*, I, 3, 1-4)

He measures the intensity of his pain through the conciseness of a flawless comparison:

> *I was as dazed as one who, smitten by the fire of Jove,*
> *Still lives and knows not that he lives.*[173]

> *Non aliter stupui, quam qui Iovis ignibus ictus*
> *Vivit et est vitae nescius ipse suae.*

> (*Tristia*, I, 3, 11-12)

The image of his sorrowful wife, who insisted on accompanying him into his exile, is constantly emphasized, like a symphonic leitmotif. His faithful Fabia is present in many of his elegies, and the poet addresses her like an always present conversation partner to

---

[172] *Ibidem*, pp. 19, 21.

[173] *Ibidem*, p. 21.

whom he confesses all his tormented feelings. Other times, he eulogizes her like a cherished deity and, to bring forward her unrivaled virtues, he resorts to his hyperbolic method – the comparison with mythological characters:

> *In uprightness neither Hector's wife excels thee*
> *Nor Laodamia, companion of her husband in death.*
> *If fate had allotted thee the Maeonian bard,*
> *Penelope's fame would be second to thine.*[174]

> *Nec probitate tua prior est aut Hectoris uxor,*
> *Aut comes extincto Laodamia viro.*
> *Tu si Maeonium vatem sortita fuisses,*
> *Penelopes esset fama secunda tuae.*

(Tristia, I, 6, 19-22)

Of all the moral qualities with which nature endowed the human soul to help him in his struggle for survival, hope is the most comforting. It accompanies us in all circumstances and follows us like our shadow, and it refuses to leave us even when the end is certain. The poet was not an exception. He often regained command of his emotions and began to have hope in people, in a change of politics, in the intervention of his friends who could, if not bring him back to Rome, at least change the location of his exile from Tomis to a place closer to his country and therefore easier to bear. We have seen how *Metamorphoses* concluded with the apotheosis of Julius Caesar and the deification of Augustus. But praise for the emperor is even more outstanding in Ovid's Pontic letters, in which the poet dedicates many pages to him. Book II of *Tristia*, composed of six hundred verses, is entirely dedicated to Augustus. If the appeals for imperial clemency did not have the anticipated effect, it was not as

---

[174]*Ibidem*, p. 37.

Publius Ovidius Naso, 43 B.C.-A.D. 17

much the fault of Augustus as of Livia, who was doing everything in her power to prevent the aging emperor from allowing himself to be overcome by compassion. Although Augustus died, followed by his plotting wife, her son Tiberius came to power, himself also filled with hatred for the exile. Thus, Ovid's letters remained null from a political point of view, but not as literature, as they made his genius endure throughout the centuries.

Tristia is followed by *Epistulae ex Ponto*, composed of four books. It was written between the years A.D. 12 and 17 (and maybe the beginning of 18). The letters are addressed to his wife Fabia, some of his friends, and influential people among the Roman aristocracy. Among the friends that he addressed were Atticus, Rufinus, and Sextus Pompeius, whom he asked to intervene at the imperial court in view of a much hoped for pardon. The tone of these entreaties is not often in agreement with what one would call "manliness," but we know that their author had become an unfortunate man crushed under the brutal blow of the emperor, a man who died as a citizen.

Because the documentary material of *Tristia* is so similar it became the basis for the elaboration of *Epistulae ex Ponto*. Thus, we shall first look at the substance of the former and later deal with its artistic valences.

Ovid wrote his letters in Tomis, where, as the poet exaggerates obsessively, "winter lasts from one year to the snow of the next winter," and where people do not drink the wine, as they do in Italy, "but they eat it like an ice cube."

> But when grim winter has thrust forth his squalid face,
> And the earth is marble-white with frost,
> And Boreas and the snow prohibit dwelling beneath
> the Bear,

His poems are fundamentally dishonest, anti-documentary tainted by his implores / yearning.

Then 'tis clear that these tribes are hard pressed by
the shivering pole.
The snow lies continuously, and once fallen, neither sun
nor rain may melt it,
For Boreas hardens and renders it eternal.
So when an earlier fall is not yet melted another has
come,
And in many places 'tis wont to remain for two years.
So mighty is the power of Aquilo, when once he is
aroused,
That he levels high towers to the ground and sweeps away
buildings.
With skins and stitched breeches they keep out of the evils
of the cold;
Of the whole body only the face is exposed.
Often their hair tinkles with hanging ice
And their beards glisten while with the mantle of frost.
Exposed wine stands upright, retaining the shape of
the jar,
And they drink, not draughts of wine, but fragments
served them![175]

At cum tristis hiems squalentia protulit ora,
Terraque marmoreo est candida facta gelu,
Nec patitur Boreas et nix habitare sub Arcto,
Tum patet has gentes axe tremente premi.
Nix iacet, et iactam ne sol pluviaeque resolvant,
Indurat Boreas perpetuamque facit.
Ergo ubi delicuit nondum prior, altera venit,
Et solet in multis bina manere Iocis;
Tantaque commoti vis est Aquilonis, ut altas
Aequet humo turres tectaque rapta ferat.

---

[175]*Ibidem*, pp. 137, 139.

Pellibus et sutis arcent mala frigora bradcis,
Oraque de toto corpore sola patent.
Saepe sonant moti glacie pedente capilli,
Et nitet inducto candida barba gelu;
Nudaque consistunt, formam servantia testae,
Vina, nec hausta meri, sed data frusta bibunt.

(*Tristia*, III, 10, 9-24)

These letters are addressed to Fabia, his wife, a few of his former friends, as well the imperial court and the two emperors, Octavian Augustus, and his successor, Tiberius. Ovid hoped in vain that these people would bring him back from his place of exile. But his fate was sealed by Livia, and the poet was not only banished, but condemned to death in the form of irrevocable exile. Even after he died, his ashes were not added to those of his Italic ancestors, but were united with those of the Getae in the midst of whom he lived his last years, surrounded by their love.

But the landscapes depicted by Ovid's pen must be interpreted with much discernment, as many of them are rendered with exaggeration. Ovid needed to emphasize the harshness of the climate and, in general, the environment in the region between the Lower Danube and the Black Sea, to stir the compassion of the emperor and thus to obtain a pardon. Despite this, his information remains the most authentic documentary source regarding the land, customs, occupations, and culture of the ancestors of the Romanians. Knowing the historical conditions in the region at the time of Ovid's exile in Tomis, it is easier to reconstruct the remote past of the Geto-Dacian people, an important component in the formation of the Romanian people.

Coming from the bright regions of the Mediterranean shores, with a generous sun and mild winters, the poet was horrified by the excessive continental climate of Scythia Minor. The cold caused Ovid to panic and he lost any notion of season, saying, for whoever wanted to believe him, that in Tomis there was no spring or summer, but only an eternal winter.

It is likely that Ovid's arrival in Tomis coincided with one of those much too long winters, but it is unlikely that during the more than eight years that he spent in exile the sun did not warm up his fragile body. It is well-known that today the Romanian shore of the Black Sea is renowned for its sun, with all its therapeutic qualities.

The hibernal season is also present in Horace's odes, but it does not have the improbable intensity of the winters described in Ovid's elegies. It is true that the latter described winter in a region farther north than the Italic regions known to the contemporary of the exiled poet. However, since we are dealing with descriptive poems, let us analyze the artistic value of the images captured by the poet and not their truthfulness:

> *Why tell of brooks frozen fast with the cold*
> *And how brittle water is dug out of the pool?*
> *The very Hister, not narrower than the papyrus-bearing*
> > *river,*
> *Mingling with the vast deep through many mouths,*
> *Freezes as the winds stiffen his dark flood,*
> *And winds its way into the sea with covered waters.*
> *Where ships had gone before now men go on foot*
> *And the waters congealed with cold feel the hoof-beat of*
> > *the horse.*
> *Across the new bridge, above the gliding current,*
> *Are drawn by Sarmatian oxen the carts of the*
> > *barbarians.*[176]

---

[176] *Ibidem*, p. 139.

Quid loquar, ut vincti concrescant frigore rivi,
Deque lacu fragiles effodiantur aquae?
Ipse, papyrifero qui non angustior amne
Miscetur vasto multa per ora freto,
Caeruleos ventis latices durantibus, Hister
Congelal et tectis in mare serpit aquis;
Quaque rates ierant, pendibus nunc itur, et undas
Frigore concretas ungula pulsat equi;
Perque novos pontes, subter labentibus undis,
Docunt Sarmatici barbara plaustra boves.

(*Tristia*, III, 10, 25-34)

No chronicle could render in such a plastic way the hibernal landscape of Scythia Minor as this elegy which, due to the rich imagination of the poet, represents a majestic painting. It is not the image of the Dobrogean winters that is contestable, but their duration, which according to the poet are endless. On the other hand, in his exile works Ovid introduces us to the ancestors of the Romanians, whose faces we would have never seen without the mirror, albeit exaggerated, of Ovid's letters.

Moreover, the poet also introduces us to the neighbors of the Getae – the Greeks, the Sarmatians, and the Scythians – whose way of life and dress he describes with true artistry. Ovid confirms the fact that the first inhabitants of Scythia Minor were the Getae, among whom there later came colonists with their commerce, as well as a few enclaves of invading peoples, like the Sarmatians and the Scythians. The Getae formed the majority of the population, as Ovid tells us, "the Getae are in a larger number." Their occupations were agriculture and raising cattle, and they formed the stable population in the region.

Returning to elegy X of *Tristia*, which reveals important evidence about the ancient territory of modern Romania, we also find

Danube.

out that the Black Sea froze over a large surface and the Hister[177]
froze in its entirety, thus offering the barbarians an opportunity to
invade Tomis, which was difficult to defend with its low wall and
only forty soldiers on the battlements.

> *So whether the cruel violence of o'er mighty Boreas*
> *Congeals the waters of the sea or the full waters of*
> > > *the river,*
> *Forthwith when the Hister has been levelled by the*
> > > *freezing Aquillo*
> *The barbarian enemy with his swift horses rides to*
> > > *the attack –*
> *An enemy strong in steeds and in far flying arrows –*
> *And lays waste far and wide the neighboring soil.*
> *Some flee, and with none to protect their lands*
> *Their unguarded resources are plundered,*
> *The small resources of the country,*
> *Flocks and creaking carts – all the wealth the poor*
> > > *peasant has.[178]*

> *Sive igitur nimii Boreae vis saeva marinas,*
> *Sive redundatas flumine cogit aquas,*
> *Protinus aequato siccis Aquilonibus Histro*
> *Invehitur celeri barbarus hostis equo;*
> *Hostis equo pollens longeque volante sagitta*
> *Vicinam late depopulatur hymum.*
> *Diffugiunt alli, nullisque tuentibus agros*
> *Incustoditae diripiuntur opes,*

---

[177]The Greek name for the Danube; the Geto-Dacian name for the river was
Dunaris.

[178]Ovid, *Tristia*, pp. 139, 141.

Ruris opens parvae, pecus et stridentia plaustra,
Et quas divitas incola pauper habet.

(*Tristia*, III, 10, 51-60)

As we can see, the image of the Scythian invasions across the frozen Hister is depicted with great poetical talent. The victims were not the inhabitants inside the city wall, but the people who lived outside of it, whose occupation was agriculture, as Ovid himself tells us. This occupation connected with the land required a stable, hard-working, and numerous population. They were the famed Getae, as Herodotus called them. Ovid describes them in detail, giving them an extensive attestation in history.

But the description of the barbarian invasions is much ampler. We learn that many natives were killed by arrows poisoned with venom or were taken into slavery, leaving behind their houses in flames. The barbarian invasions left barren lands behind, and many years would pass before new settlements appeared.

Ovid's information is credible, and the recent archeological discoveries made in Dobrogea confirm it to a great extent. At the end of the elegy, however, the poet adds a few exaggerations to impress his readers:

Not here the sweet grape lying hidden in the leafy shade
Nor the frothing must be brimming the deep vats!
Fruits are denied in this region nor here would Acontius
*   have anything*
On which to write the words for his sweetheart to read.
One may see naked fields, leafless, treeless –
A place, alas! no fortunate man should visit.[179]

---

[179]*Ibidem*, p. 141.

Non hic pampinea dulcis latet uva sub umbra,
Nec cumulant altos fervida musta lacus.
Poma negat regio, nec haberet Acontius in quo
Scriberet hic dominae verba legenda suae.
Aspiceres nudos sine fronde, sine arbore, campos:
Heu loca felici non adeunda viro!

(*Tristia*, III, 10, 71-75).

A somber and unreal image. If the must was not "brimming the deep vats," then what were the numerous wine presses discovered in Dobrogea used for? And what inspired the artists of the time to decorate so many monuments with grape clusters and leaves? And why was the Greek city south of Callatis – today's Balcic – named Dionysopolis?

Also, there is no truth in the affirmation about the inexistence of fruit trees, because today, as in ancient times, many fruit trees are planted on the territory between the Lower Danube and the Black Sea, especially in the north and south (however, the orchards did not reach the gates of the city where the poet lived in exile).

Ovid's references to the population of Tomis, as well as to various sedentary tribes around it, can be found in most of his letters in *Tristia* and *Epistulae ex Ponto*. Unfortunately, as the poet was trying to impress and not to inform his reader, he limited himself to simple, superficial sketches, avoiding or ignoring information that would be of interest regarding the extraction, place, time, religion, and way of life of the respective people. Nevertheless, the information gathered from Ovid's work represents a confirmation of the ethnic continuity of the Romanian people in the geographical space that it has occupied from antiquity until today. We repeat, some of Ovid's information concerning the Getae are not true. In light of archeological discoveries, we know for certain that the Getae were at a high stage of civilization, although certainly not more advanced than the Greeks or the Romans.

But let us allow the eyewitness poet to speak about the inhabitants of Tomis and their neighbors:

> *What the people of the land of Tomis are like,*
> *Amid what customs I live, are you interested to know?*
> *Though upon this coast there is a mixture of Greeks*
>   *and Getae,*
> *It derives more from the scarce pacified Getae.*[180]

> *Turba Tomitanae quae sit regionis et inter*
> *Quos habitem mores, discere cura tibi est?*
> *Mixta sit haec quamvis inter Graecosque Getasque,*
> *A male pacatis plus trahit ora Getis.*

                    (*Tristia*, V, 7, 9-12)

It results that the Greeks in Tomis were living side by side with the Getae, making commercial exchanges, meeting at the circus, at the theater, etc. During this time, however, beyond the city walls, other tribes of Getae and Sarmatians attacked and pillaged:

> *Greater hordes of Sarmatae and Getae go and come*
> *Upon their horses along the road. Among them*
> *There is not one who does not bear quiver and bow,*
> *And darts yellow with viper's gall.*
> *Harsh voices, grim faces, surest indication of their minds,*
> *Neither hair nor beard trimmed by practised hand,*
> *Right hands not slow to stab and wound with the knife*
> *Which every barbarian wears fastened to his side.*[181]

---

[180] *Ibidem*, p. 237.

[181] *Ibidem*, p. 237.

Sarmaticae maior Gericaeque frequentia gentis
Per medias in equis itque reditque vias.
In quibus est nemo, qui non coryton et arcum
Telaque vipereo lurida felle gerat.
Vox fera, trux vultus, verissima mentis imago,
Non coma, non trita barba resecta manu,
Dextera non segnis fixo dare vulnera cultro,
Quem iunctum lateri barbarus omnis habet.

(*Tristia*, V, 7, 13-20)

The letters contained in *Tristia* were written during the first part of Ovid's exile in Tomis and that is why his feelings of horror and desperation are extremely virulent. His contempt for the barbarians can be explained through the harsh nature of the natives with whom he came into contact, who were irascible and always ready to argue.

There is no sign in any of Ovid's letters that he was inclined to bravery, but since, in Tomis. he would put on his helmet and be prepared to climb upon the battlements if necessary, he did it out of stringent necessity. On the other hand, he tells us that he was not in good relations with the Getae. This is again an exaggeration, proven by his own verses, which show the exact opposite:

Here it is that I am a barbarian, understood by nobody;
The Getae laugh stupidly at Latin words, and in my
                                                    presence
They often talk maliciously about me in perfect security,
Perchance reproaching me with my exile.
Naturally they think that I am poking fun at them
Whenever I have nodded no or yes to their speech.[182]

---

[182]*Ibidem*, p. 249.

Barbarus hic ego sum, qui non intellegor ulli
Et rident stolidi verba Latina Getae;
Meque palam de me tuto mala saepe loquuntur,
Forsitan obiciunt exilliumque mihi.
Utque fit, in se aliquid fingi, dicentibus illis
Abnuerim quotiens adnuerimque, putant.

(*Tristia*, V, 10, 37-42)

A virtuous side of the Getae is revealed here, that of hospitality, suggestively expressed by Ovid.

Reading *Epistulae ex Ponto* we shall see that, although Ovid's laments continue, they are less desperate in comparison with those in *Tristia*. The poet became accustomed to his situation or began to resign himself to his fate. While, at first, he could not accept the thought of living among the Getae, now he began to learn their language and, toward the end of his life, he would even take pride in being "the greatest poet on the banks of the Danube." He became more benevolent toward his hosts as his hopes for repatriation faded; despite all the letters he sent to Rome, none of them brought him an encouraging answer. Augustus died and was succeeded by Tiberius, from whom the exiled poet could not hope for anything. His exile continued. In the letters, he sent to Rome we find the same pessimism and it is seldom that we uncover new details.

The fate of the poet remained the same and he began to accept the fact that it would never change.

In line with his new views concerning the Getae, in the second letter of book I of *Epistulae ex Ponto,* we find out that the Getae were a warlike people, resistant to privations:

The most of these people neither care for thee, fair Rome,
Nor fear the arms of Ausonian soldiery.
Bows and full quiver lend them courage,

And horses capable of marches however lengthy
And the knowledge how to ensure for long both thirst
                                    and hunger,
And that a pursuing enemy will have no water.[183]

Maxima pars hominum, nec te, pulcherrima, curat,
Roma, nec Ausonii militis arma timet.
Dant illis animas arcus plenaeque pharetrae
Quamque libet longis cursibus aptus equus,
Quodque sitim didicere diu tolerare famemque,
Quodque sequens nullas hostis habebit aquas.

(*Epistulae ex Ponto*, I, 2, 83-88)

Finally, we can gather some precious information about some of their occupations, with important social implications:

Often has the gleam of purple bordered your robe,
But there is no such dye as that by the Sarmatian sea.

The flocks produce a coarse fleece and the daughters
                                    of Tomis
Have not learned the craft of Pallas.
Instead of working the wool they grind Ceres' gifts
Or carry heavy burdens of water supported on their
                                    heads.[184]

Purpura saepe tuos fulgens praetexit amictus.
Sed non Sarmatico tingitur illa mari
Vellera dura ferunt pecudes, et Palladis uti.
Arte Tomitanae non didicere nurus.

---

[183] *Ibidem*, pp. 275, 277.

[184] *Ibidem*, p. 419.

Femina pro lana Cerealia munera frangit,
Suppositoque gravem vertice portat aquam.

(*Epistulae ex Ponto*, III, 8, 7-12)

In their turn, the people of Tomis showed care and love for the suffering poet – sentiments expressed suggestively in the verses of Ovid's letter to Rufinus:

Your gentle harboring of my fate, Tomitae,
Shows how kindly are men of Grecian stock.
My own people, the Paeligni, my home country of Sulmo
Could not have been gentler to my woes.
An honour which you would scarcely grant to one
Who was without blemish and secure, that you have
                          recently granted to me:
I am as yet the only one immune upon your shores,
Those only excepted who have the boon by law.
My brow has been veiled with a sacred chaplet
Which the popular favour placed there all against my will.
Wherefore dear as is to Latona the land of Delos,
Which alone offered her a safe place in her wandering,
So dear is Tomis to me; to me exiled from my native
                          abode
It remains hospitable and loyal to the present time.[185]

Molliter a vobis mea sors excepta, Tomitae,
Tam mites Graios indicat esse viros.
Gens mea Paeligni regioque domestica Sulmo
Non potuit nostris tenior esse malis.
Quem vix incolumi cuiquam salvoque daretis,
Is datus a vobis est mihi nuper honor.
Solus adhuc ego sum vestris immunis in oris,

---

[185]*Ibidem*, pp. 481, 483.

Exceptis, siqui munera legis habent.
Tempora sacrata mea sunt velata corona,
Publicus invito quam favor imposuit.
Quam grata est igitur Latonae Delia tellus,
Erranti tutum quae dedit una locum,
Tam mihi cara Tomis, patria quae sede fugatis
Tempus ad hoc nobis hospital fida manet.

(*Epistulae ex Ponto*, IV, 14, 47-60)

Reading the first elegies it is not difficult to sense the disdain of the hosts toward their unusual guest, a sentiment which disappeared later and was replaced by friendship between them. This was aided by the fact as the years passed and no sign of an annulment of his banishment came from Rome, the only thing left for Ovid to do was to resign himself to his fate. Thus, he began to make friends with the Getae, sharing their joys, learning their language, and, because he wanted to prove how close he was to them, writing a poem in their language. But, unfortunately, this unique literary product in the Getic language was lost. It is possible that the survival of this piece would have rivalled the discovery of the Rosetta Stone, thanks to which Champollion was able to decipher the enigmas of Egyptian hieroglyphics.

During his exile, Ovid also wrote a poem in Greek, entitled *Halieutica*, which remained unfinished. In this opuscule, the poet gives information on different species of fish, such as the sturgeon and the sea wolf. He also provides biological details concerning the continuous battles among the species, their attack and defense methods, and the laws that govern the world of animals. The elaboration of this poetical-scientific work proves that the poet from Sulmo had acquired a solid education during his studies in Rome, thanks to which he knew how to master the iambuses, the trochees, and the dactyls, but also the elements necessary for scientific study.

Halieutica also shows Ovid as a connoisseur of Homer's language, since he ventured to write a poem in it.

Finally, also in Tomis, Ovid wrote *Ibis*, in elegiac distich, composed of about six hundred verses. The work dates from the first five years of his exile and consists of invectives and imprecations addressed to an unknown enemy, named conventionally Ibis. The work is on the same line with the iambuses of Archilloch[186] and the letter with the same title signed by Callimachus.[187] Here, as in most of his writings, Ovid appeals to mythological material, wishing upon his enemies the misfortunes endured by certain legendary and mythological heroes.

The banishment of the unfortunate poet from Sulmo lasted until the end of his life. Old and ill, Ovid was no longer waiting for his return to his country, but for his death, for whose greeting he wrote the sad epitaph, now engraved on the marble of the pedestal that supports his statue in Constanţa:

> *I, who lie here, with render loves once played,*
> *Naso, the bard, whose life his wit betrayed.*
> *Grudge not, a lover, as though passest by,*
> *A prayer: "Soft may the bones of Naso lie!"*

> *Hic ego qui jaceo tenerorum lusor amorum*
> *Ingenio perri Naso poeta meo*
> *At tibi qui transis ne sit grave quisquis amasti*
> *Dicere Nasonis molliter ossa cubent.*

The characteristic of this quatrain lies in the kindness and gentleness of the one who wrote it: no sign of anger or vanity; the poet died as he lived, loving his talent with obstinacy and looking

---

[186] *Scriitori greci şi latini…*, see Archiloch and Calimachus.

[187] *Ibidem.*

kindly at those who would come to visit his grave. To his wife, Fabia, he had expressed his wish to have his remains taken to Rome. This document, however, does not tell us whether his wish was fulfilled. In his verses, the poet does not exclude the possibility of his burial in a tomb in Tomis:

> *May I lie entombed in the sands of Tomis.*[188]

> *Inque Tomitana iaceam tumulatus harena.*

> (*Epistulae ex Ponto*, 1, 6, 49)

Indeed, he died in the year A.D. 17 and was buried with honor by the people of Tomis – *ante oppidi portam* – at the gate of the city. Of course, he died alone, but he was consoled by the thought that he would survive through his work. Today, Ovid lives on in the memory of all of humanity and his name represents the glory of the entire Latin race, and, therefore, of the Romanian people as well.

---

[188]*Tristia/Epistulae Ex Ponto*, p. 299.

CHAPTER VI

POST-OVIDIAN TOMIS

Almost two thousand years have passed since the death of the poet who was sacrificed by the ambitions of an autocrat at the beginning of an empire. The small city of Tomis, which received him with hospitality, became his final resting place. Ovid's remains became one with the earth of his adoptive land.

Now let us follow the historical account of this place from the time when the days of the Latin poet ended up to modern times and, passing through decades, centuries, and millennia, to observe the changes that have taken place. Of course, we must keep in mind Ovid's work in exile, because the people and places that he knew can still be recognized, despite the changes that have taken place. Tomis, at the beginning of the Christian era, underwent amazing transformations over its long journey through time. Often it disappears into the past, obscured by a lack of information, only to reappear again, bigger and brighter – always on the same territory of the promontory on which, two thousand five hundred years ago, the Miletian Greeks began living next to the Getae, gradually replacing the earthen huts with stone walls.

The bard exiled in Tomis, with his *Letters from Pontus*, identifies himself with the beginning of the Roman period in this region and with the time when the Romanian people were beginning to form on the shores of the sea, out of an ethnic mixture to which Ovid was a witness.

Thus, after the year 29 B.C., the shore of Scythia Minor became Roman patrimony, with all the implications resulting from a domination specific to an army already experienced in conquering and ruling foreign territories. The Greeks in Tomis, whose occupations had been for centuries commerce and navigation, were in good relations with Rome, since the similarity of their cultures brought them closer and did not divide them as had happened not long before.

Romanization began – more exactly the adaptation of the new city to the new conditions of life and social and economic practices specific to Rome – but given the traditional Hellenic characteristic of the cities of Histria, Tomis, and Callatis, this did not exclude anything that was Greek. Especially in spiritual life, fusions, contaminations, and adaptations of beliefs, customs, and funeral practices took place – many of these being tributary to Ovid himself, whose memory lives in the conscience of the generations that followed. *Hic ego qui jaceo*... are the words engraved on many funerary stones in the following centuries.

In the year A.D. 46, Ripa Thraciae was integrated into the province of Moesia, and following the reforms of Domitian of the year A.D. 86, two new administrative and military entities appeared along the Danube: Moesia Superior and Moesia Inferior – modern Dobrogea being included in the latter. Tomis was the residence of the province, of the *praefectura* of the Pontic shore, of the religious community constituted on the basis of the interests of survival in the ever more extensive Latin world, of the Greek cities of Pentapolis,[189] later called Hexapolis (Histria, Tomis, Callatis, Odessos, Dionysopolis, and Messembria)

This community preserved the old social-administrative institutions of the Greeks such as the council of elders and the popular assembly, the cults and practices inherent to these institutions, their economic occupations. Beginning with the second century A.D., Tomis became a true metropolis of the Pontus Euxinus, attested as such by numerous literary, archeological, epigraphic, and numismatic documents discovered in modern times over the entire territory of the old city.

The prosperity of Tomis increased during the Antonine Dynasty in the second century A.D., the final consolidation of Roman power on the Lower Danube being achieved under the eminent Emperor Marcus Ulpius Trajanus (A.D. 98-117). Great accomplishments are tied to his name: the foundations of the Danubian *limes,*[190] the great triumphal monument at Adamclisi, which commemorates, just like Trajan's Column in Rome, the conquest of Dacia, the establishment of impressive villages, cities, and fortresses.

Tomis prospered, especially in its commerce. Its relations with the Pontic-Aegean and Mediterranean world increased, its merchants travelling to important cities like Byzantium,[191] Cyzicos,[192]

---

[189] *Dicţionarul de istorie veche a României*, see Pentapolis.

[190] *Ibidem*, see *limes Scythicus*.

[191] *Ibidem*, see *Bizanţ*.

[192] A city in Propontida (on the Sea of Marmara) of great economic importance. Histria and Tomis began having economic relations with this city early on, the coins issued in its mints having a wide circulation here in antiquity. *Dicţionar de istorie veche…*, see *Cyzic*.

Palmyra,[193] Smyrna,[194] Athens,[195] Nicomedia,[196] Ancyra,[197] and others. From the Danubian areas and those of Roman Dacia, immense quantities of goods came by land which brought important revenues to the city of Tomis.

In the rural interior of the city, new properties appeared that belonged to colonists arriving from the empire: these properties were the *villae rusticae*[198] and *praedia*,[199] with important production destined for consumption, but especially for commerce. Numerous neighboring villages – *vici* – assured agricultural production and the labor force. At the same time, they represented points of intense cohabitation between the Romans and the native population. The latter are mentioned in inscriptions with names like Areibalos, Deospor, Mucasius, Seuthes, Decibalus, etc.[200]

The colonists, veterans, and Roman soldiers who came to the city of Tomis and the area around it caused ethnic fusions to which new forms of culture, language, and religion inherently correspond. The region was penetrated by new cults and deities, especially Oriental ones, such as Cybele,[201] Mithra,[202] Isis, Attis,[203] and others.

---

[193]The kingdom of Palmyra, with the homonymous city, in the Near East.

[194]The ancient name of today's city of Izmir in Turkey.

[195]*Encyclopedia civilizaţiei greceşti*, Bucureşti, 1970, see *Atena*.

[196]City in Bythinia, Asia Minor.

[197]The ancient name of the city of Ankara, the capital of Turkey.

[198]*Dicţionar de istorie veche…*, see *villa*.

[199]An agricultural unit belonging to Roman colonists or to veterans.

[200]I.I. Russu, *Limba traco-dacilor*, Bucureşti, 1967, passim.

[201]Anca Balaci, *op.cit.*, see *Cybela*

[202]*Dicţionar de istorie veche…*, see Mithras.

[203]Anca Balaci, *op.cit.*, see Attis.

But the local deities were also maintained. The native cult of the Thracian Knight[204] was practiced, both in urban as well as rural sanctuaries, proving its popularity. Of the temples that existed, only a few stone and marble ruins have survived until today. The inscriptions discovered also mention Greco-Roman deities: Poseidon, Dionysus, Apollo, Dioscuri, Diana,[205] etc. Important works of art correspond to this wide range of deities. Among the 24 sculpted monuments discovered in 1962, the following distinguish themselves through their refinement and execution: *Fortuna with Pontos* (protectors of the city),[206] *Snake Glycon, The Aedicula with the double Nemesis, Isis, The Thracian Knight, Hecate,*[207] etc., all dating from the first and the second centuries A.D. To these we add the huge marble sarcophaguses, like that of an *agoranom,*[208] worshiper of the god Men,[209] the statue of the *Citizen of Tomis,* and so many others, all of them testimonies of high quality local artistic practices, both laic and religious.

This *Pax Romana* was followed by a long period of crisis, with important implications in all the fields: social, economic, political, etc. In the middle of the third century A.D., barbarians penetrated the northeastern borders of the empire: military anarchy overtook Rome, with the soldiers offering the imperial purple to their commanders. These internal struggles had repercussions throughout the empire.

---

[204] *Dicționar de istorie veche…*, see Cavalerul trac.

[205] Anca Balaci, *op.cit.,* all the deities mentioned above.

[206] *Tezaurul de sculpturi de la Tomis*, Constanța, 1963, pp. 16-24

[207] *Ibidem.*

[208] *Dicționar de istorie,* see *agoranom.*

[209] *Ibidem.*

In the year A.D. 238, the Carps[210] and the Goths[211] attacked and destroyed the region at the mouth of the Danube. They were confronted by powerful armies, commanded by emperors and skillful generals, who repelled them with difficulty. Plundering, fires, and other calamities succeeded each other in short intervals. In A.D. 239, Tomis was besieged on water and on land by the Goths and the Heruls[212] and resisted, with difficulty, due to its powerful walls and, probably, due to subterranean tunnels that enabled the provisioning of the population and the movement of the troops. Economic life was seriously affected. During the time of Phillip the Arab (A.D. 245-249), the minting of new coins ceased. This was a sign that the great metropolis would fall. But that did not happen. During the reigns of Emperor Aurelian (A.D. 270-275) and his successors the empire began to recover. The wars with the barbarians – *bellum Scythicum* – came to an end, villages and cities were rebuilt, and the borders reestablished. Diocletian (A.D. 284-305) restored peace through reforms applied at a military, administrative, and economic level. Prosperity resumed, beginning in the fourth century A.D., under Constantine the Great (A.D. 306-337). The new name of the region between the Danube and the Black Sea was, beginning with Diocletian, Scythia, with its capital at Tomis.

The capital of the empire moved to Constantinople, and its vicinity gave Tomis vital economic impulses, transforming it into an important provisioning center for the new imperial city. This assertion is supported by the example of the great edifice with mosaic built in the fourth century A.D. in the agora of Tomis. In fact, an intense building activity took place in the city, but there were also

---

[210] *Ibidem*, see *carpi*.

[211] *Ibidem*, see *goți*.

[212] *Ibidem*.

moments of panic (Zosimos, *Contemporary History*, IV, 40). These were caused by attacks by the Goths, like those during the reign of Valens (A.D. 364-378), an emperor who died in battle at Adrianople in A.D. 378. Many barbarians were now settled along the Danube to defend the border, but this strategy did not prove very successful, because the plundering attacks did not cease. This is the context of the incident recounted by Zosimos concerning the Gothic attack on Tomis in A.D. 386, which was repelled by an act of great bravery by the commander of the fortress, Gerontius.

Another author (Sozomenos, *Church History*, VI, 21, 2) presents Tomis in the fifth century A.D. as a large city, with a prosperous and renowned episcopal center, as a result of the policy of tolerance initiated by Constantine the Great. Many Christian churches were built here, some of them impressive in their dimensions and their crypts. The great basilica with *martyrium*,[213] considered to have been the archiepiscopal seat, next to two other basilicas, and the painted crypt are testimonies that prove the importance of Tomis in comparison with other ecclesiastical centers in the region. We mention here the participation of certain representatives of the clergy from Tomis at different ecumenical synods. The documents of the time give the names of bishops who intervened energetically in the dogmatic disputes that condemned Arianism. From Tomis, Christianity spread north of the Danube, and also among the Goths and the Huns.

A treasure discovered in Tomis attests to the name of Bishop Paternus, "metropolitan of the province of Scythia,"[214] whose descendants also became great ecclesiastical personalities. The documents mention the preeminent position of Tomis in the

---

[213] *Ibidem*, see *martyrium*.

[214] *Ibidem*, see *Paternus*.

Christian Orthodox world for many centuries. Next to the religious edifices, there appeared numerous laic buildings as well, due to certain emperors who were trying to rebuild the empire. Procopius of Caesarea mentions that during the time of Justinian (A.D. 527-565), fortresses and cities were being rebuilt throughout the province, one of these being Tomis. During that period, the butcher's guild rebuilt, at their own expense, a portion of the defensive wall with a tower, a fact attested to by an inscription engraved in stone on this occasion, which can still be read today.

The Roman-Byzantine Empire, exhausted by the continuous wars of Justinian, could hardly resist barbarian attacks any longer. Between A.D. 566 and 602 decisive battles took place with the Avars[215] and the Slavs.[216] Besieged in A.D. 599, Tomis resisted with difficulty. At the beginning of the next century, the Slavs occupied the region – only the shore still remained under Byzantine rule. The Bulgars struck the decisive blow[217] in their hasty advance southward, attracted by Byzantine riches.

That was how the Roman and Roman-Byzantine epoch of Tomis and of the entire province ended, whose beginnings merged with the destiny of the exiled poet. A domination that lasted for over seven centuries came to an end. Despite its obsolete socio-economic forms, it had created a new people, with different customs, beliefs, and occupations. They were the ancestors of the Romanians at the middle of the millennium, who had already become an ethnic reality. The Pontic Romanians heroically confronted the waves of new

---

[215]*Ibidem*, see *avari*.

[216]*Ibidem*, see *slavi*.

[217]*Ibidem*, see *bulgari*.

migrations by the Pechenegs,[218] the Uzi,[219] the Cumans,[220] and the Tartars;[221] they were closely tied to the civilization guarded by the Byzantine royal eagle of Tsarigrad,[222] which they supplied with products from their lands by the Lower Danube on the ships of Genoese merchants, in Vicina,[223] Lykostomion,[224] Constantia, Pangalia (Mangalia), etc. The chronicles recorded heroic deeds of unequaled bravery and courage like those performed by the Basarabs[225] and the Muşats,[226] by Mircea the Old and Stephen the Great, by John Hunyadi[227] and Michael the Brave,[228] by all the

---

[218] *Ibidem*, see *pecenegi*.

[219] *Ibidem*, see *uzi*.

[220] *Ibidem*, see *cumani*.

[221] *Ibidem*, see *tătari*.

[222] The Slavic name of Byzantium.

[223] An important economic center on the Lower Danube, probably the center of the duchy ruled by Satza in the tenth century. It has not yet been identified, but investigations are ongoing.

[224] A medieval city in the Danube Delta, modern Chilia, of great economic importance during the thirteenth and fourteenth centuries. After that it disappeared, most likely because of the sanding caused by the alluvial deposits carried by the Danube into the sea. It appears that modern Chilia is not located in the exact same spot as old Lykostomion.

[225] A long dynasty in Wallachia, inaugurated by Basarab I (c. 1310-1352); the most important ruler of this dynasty was Mircea the Old (1386-1418).

[226] A Moldavian dynasty between the fourteenth and sixteenth centuries which gave Moldavia some great rulers, one of whom was Stephen the Great (1457-1504).

[227] Voievod of Transylvania (1441-1456) and governor of Hungary.

[228] Voievod of Wallachia between 1593-1601; he defended the freedom and independence of the country, winning many victories over the Ottomans. He was the first to unite the three Romanian principalities – Wallachia, Moldavia, and Transylvania – in 1600.

Wallachian, Moldavian, and Transylvanian voivodes who fought with their swords against the Ottomans to protect their freedom.

Nevertheless, the most powerful empire of the time, the Ottomans, who ruled over all of the Balkan Peninsula, took possession of Dobrogea as well. They remained here for almost four and a half centuries. Medieval history is strewn with the testimonies of the struggles and sufferings of a people who, maintaining their identity untouched by vicissitudes, would eventually emerge victorious.

The War for Independence in 1877 brought Romania, besides autonomy and sovereignty, the right to rule over that part of the country with its opening to the sea, the land of Burebista, Decebal, Trajan, and Mircea the Old. On 23 November 1878, after the Congress of Berlin, Ovid's beautiful city, *Küstendje*, as it had been called by the Ottomans, regained its name of Latin origin, Constanţa.

The millenary city is today the second largest in Romania. It grew throughout the centuries, but its heart has always been the peninsula that closes, in the northeast, the gulf port. The port has always been the reason for and the basis of the development of Constanţa. Around the gulf, where in ancient times ships halted, carried there by sails or by the oars of convicts, a gradual architectural and renewal process has been taking place, raising the city to new heights.

CHAPTER VII

OVID AND POSTERITY

Undoubtedly, *Metamorphoses* represents Ovid's most important work, both through its beauty, as well as through its implications for world literature. Few of the great literary works of antiquity have had such a great influence on men of letters as this collection of wonderful stories has had. These myths and legends were also treated by other Greek and Latin artists, but none of them gained Ovid's popularity and fame. Ovid understood that it is not enough to write beautifully just for a restricted category of readers, but that he must elaborate his work so that it attracted the interest of the entire world. Since the beginning of his literary activity, Ovid wrote for everyday readers, not only for restricted circles. He sensed that this was necessary for his work to become not only perennial, but also universal.

A special place in Ovid's work is occupied by the two collections of elegies: *Tristia* and *Epistulae ex Ponto*, works whose substance originates from authentic lyricism. In these works, the author sings of his love, laments his pain, and expresses his hope for a future rehabilitation. But the question arises: without the pain of his exile in Tomis would these two masterpieces of world literature have been born? Ovid's Pontic elegies are a gift to humanity, which has loved, cried, and hoped. These feelings are the true sources of lyrical poetry.

Ovid's works are poetical creations of undeniable quality, as they manage to attain the highest goal: they communicate aesthetic emotion to the reader and give humanity a new message. They move us and overwhelm us.

Critics have reproached Ovid for using rhetoric in *Tristia* and *Epistulae ex Ponto*. This is true. But let us examine how he uses rhetoric: in his pleas to the emperors to commute his sentence; in the description of the dramatic moments caused by the parting from his family; when he implores his friends to intervene with the imperial court on his behalf, etc. Often convincing someone requires the exaggeration of certain situations. This is why the rhetoric in Ovid's elegies should not be considered a flaw in his poetic technique, but a method of self-analysis, in which persuasive accents are justified.

We mentioned earlier another condition for a true artist, namely that of providing humanity with a new message, which Ovid fulfilled. What is the personal message that the poet from Sulmo addressed to us? It is an invitation to love. Ovid looks at women in a new light; he becomes their confessor and speaks about them with affection and a great deal of understanding. We can say that, through his gentleness, Ovid announced the appearance in world literature of Petrarch, Dante, Alfred de Musset, and even of the Romanian national poet Mihai Eminescu.

Few ancient poets have inspired, in the two thousand years since his death, as many other poets as has Publius Ovidius Naso. This phenomenon confirms his power of seduction. Due to imitators, but especially to translations and authentic artists who reconsidered his material, Ovid entered the circuit of universal values. Various allegorical interpretations appeared during the Middle Ages with the moralizing finality of the stories in *Metamorphoses*, Ovid's most widely read and influential work.

Representatives of Medieval French literature, such as Chrétien de Troyes,[229] Guillaume de Lorris,[230] and Jean de Meung, were very familiar with Ovid's work.[231] Ovid's *Metamorphoses* and *Fasti* were the favorite works of the English Medieval poet Geoffrey Chaucer,[232] author of the famous *Canterbury Tales*, who considered them to be of great aesthetic value. But Ovid's poetry was most popular during the Renaissance period.

The famous pre-Renaissance poet Petrarch, addressing Laura, uses Ovidian means of expression. Due to its mythological erudition and literary craftsmanship, *Metamorphoses* was very much appreciated by the humanists of the Renaissance in Italy, France, and England. In France, for example, Joachim de Bellay[233] and Pierre de Ronsard[234] were the most fervent admirers of Ovid. They imitated and adapted Ovidian motifs in their poetical works. In England, the great William Shakespeare, who was considered the pinnacle of the entire Renaissance in Western Europe, used Ovidian motifs in his

---

[229]A French poet from the twelfth century, whose works were inspired from Latin authors. Most of his works were lost, with the exception of *Filomena* and the novels *Aeneas* and the *Aeneid, Lancelot,* etc.

[230]He lived in the thirteenth century and is the author of the first part of *Roman de la Rose.*

[231]French writer (1240-1305) who wrote the second part of *Roman de la Rose.*

[232]Geoffrey Chaucer (1340-1400), English poet and man of letters, founder of English national literature.

[233]French poet who, together with Ronsard, founded the group of the Pleiad.

[234]French poet and writer (1524-1585), leader of the Pleiad; he wrote sonnets collected in the volume *Amours*, followed by *Continuation des Amours, Amour pour Hélène,* etc.

sonnets and also in his play *A Midsummer Night's Dream*. The English bard based this play on the legend of Pyramus and Thisbe and that of Actaeon, and he transformed its heroes according to the Ovidian model. In German literature, great writers like Goethe and Schiller benefited from the inexhaustible Ovidian spirit. The legend of Faust, with his transformation at the command of a witch, seems to have sprung from *Metamorphoses*.

***

The great personality of Ovid persisted on the territory of his exile, taking various forms in the view of the generations that followed him, often being amplified to legendary dimensions, of which scholars must be extremely circumspect.

Be it legendary or even distorted information, resulting from the difficult historical circumstances of the place, we should still present it succinctly, to help the reader understand the influence of Ovid in the centuries after his death in Tomis.

We know that Ovid died in Tomis in the year A.D. 17. The only information we have worthy of credence is in the work of Eusebius of Caesarea,[235] but whose *Chronicle* suffered interpolations made later by another ecclesiastical writer, Hieronymus (A.D. 345-420). In short, the chronicle relates:

> In the year A.D. 17, during 198th Olympic Games, the poet Ovid died in exile and was buried near the city of Tomis.

> [Anno 17 p.H. CXCVIII Olymp. Ovidius poeta in exilio diem obiit et iuxta oppidum Tomos sepelitur.]

---

[235]Ecclesiastical writer (A.D. 240-340). His chronicle was continued and translated in Greek by Hieronymus. Around the year A.D. 325, he wrote a *Church History* and afterwards *The Life of Emperor Constantine.*

Later literary sources, which include Georgios Trapezuntius,[236] a Greek monk who taught in Venice, and to Caelius Rhodiginus,[237] a Humanist writer from the beginning of the sixteenth century, both based apparently on information gathered from the work of the monk Planudes[238] from the thirteenth century, tell us that not only was Ovid honored by the people of Tomis during his lifetime, but that after the poet's death they built a burial place for him worthy of admiration, which they placed at the gate of the city. It is difficult to assess the accuracy of this information. But until proof to the contrary, or an archeological discovery on which we could draw conclusions, we must give this information serious consideration.

Where could this wall have been, with its gate? There is no indication, no matter how vague, that archeologists can use. We can only suspect that, at the time of Ovid's exile in Tomis, the rather small Hellenic precinct still functioned, if we consider that it could be defended only by forty soldiers commanded by two *hegemons*. Its boundaries could have followed the dividing line between the peninsula and the continental area of today's city, admitting that the small *polis* – using Strabo's definition of the term – occupied only the promontory.

To look for Ovid's grave here, be it an imposing sarcophagus or just a sepulchral urn, is impossible for two reasons: first, the strata of the civilizations has been disturbed so much and so deeply in modern times that the archeological elements, regardless of their epoch, have been completely destroyed; second, the building of the different cities in their chronological succession, culminating with the modern

---

[236]N. Lascu, "Ovidiu în România," in *Publius Ovidus Naso*, Bucureşti, 1957, p. 345.

[237]*Ibidem.*

[238]*Ibidem.*

city of Constanţa, over the precincts of ancient Tomis, makes systematic research impossible.

Perhaps the traditions and legends concerning Constanţa could lead to some answers, and a few initial steps have been made in this direction. Despite their failure, two recent episodes are worth mentioning, relating the interest of people in modern times to discover the funeral relic of the great Latin poet.

As the centuries-long Ottoman domination on the Lower Danube came to an end and the peoples of the Balkans began to demand their right to freedom and independence, wars between Tsarist Russia and the Ottoman Empire for domination over the mouth of the Danube broke out. This gradually helped to create the conditions for the formation of a united Romanian national state. The Crimean War, from 1853 to 1856,[239] presented the opportunity for·the union of Moldavia and Wallachia.

From Dobrogea, English and French ships, loaded with archeological monuments from Tomis and its surroundings, sailed toward the great museums of the West. Nevertheless, the spoliation, a result of the dramatic circumstances of the time, had a scientific results of great importance for the Romanians: the Greek and Latin inscriptions, arriving in the hands of scientific authorities like Thomas Mommsen,[240] calculated the topography of ancient Tomis

---

[239]The war fought between 1853 and 1856 between Russia, on one side, and Turkey, England, France, and Sardinia on the other, the purpose of the latter being to extend their areas of influence and to support the Ottoman Empire which was in full decline. Prior to the siege of the city of Sevastopol, in the Crimea, where the military operations were of great intensity, the armies of the allies were quartered in Constanţa, but, because the plague decimated their troops, the battlefield moved northward.

[240]German historian and philologist of international fame, he wrote *A Roman History, The History of the Roman Coin, A Textbook of the Antiquity*, etc. His

on the territory of the former village of Anadolkioi,[241] near Küstendje (Constanţa). Based on this, foreign and Romanian scholars – among them Grigore Tocilescu deserves special mention – concluded, around 1880, that Constanţa itself is built exactly on the territory of ancient Tomis. This incontestable scientific information brought all the previous disputes to an end, and established the exact place of Ovid's city of exile, and the new historical conditions, resulting from the integration of Dobrogea within the natural borders of Romania immediately following the War for Independence in 1877, allowed for extensive archeological and historical investigations, which produced exceptional results.

Ovid received a great deal of attention: the Romanians and the Italians searched for his footsteps in the old city and around it, in traditions, customs, and stories. The emulation justified by the enthusiasm of the rebirth and unification of a young and vigorous people, with a past strongly connected to the Geto-Dacians and the Romans, became a moral foundation of a patriotic belief for the generations of the time.

In 1880, the prefect of Constanţa, Remus Opreanu, came up with the idea of raising a statue of Ovid in the city that had just been identified with the ancient Tomis. Grigore Tocilescu, giving course to some categorical imperatives of the time, elaborated an extensive plan for research at Adamclisi and for the organization of a large museum in Constanţa. At the same time, a man of vast culture and a

---

name is connected to the famous *Corpus inscriptionum latinarum*, on which he worked for years as editing director.

[241]Former Turkish village, now an important district of the city of Constanţa, whose name means "the village of the Anatolians."

great friend of the Romanians, the Italian Bruto Amante,[242] from Naples, came to Constanța to trace the steps of Ovid.

Bruto Amante had heard of "an island of Ovid." Together with his host in Constanța, in 1884, he made a trip to the island in the middle of Lake Siutghiol, near a place called Canara, today a town called Ovidiu, being convinced that the stories told by the Turkish villagers, as well as the name of the island, could place him on the traces of the poet. This is what the Italian visitor wrote:

> On the island, which belongs to Ibraim Effendi and where probably no merchant has ever entered, a strange spectacle appears before your eyes. Hundreds of eagles and thousands of ravens and wild pigeons are circling in the air, forming a dome above the bushes. The branches are covered by a great number of these inhabitants and their cries are so loud and unbearable that it is impossible to stay long on the island. The trees are mainly very old oaks, a few wild pear trees, and there are also a few grape vines on which I noticed extremely small grapes; the ground is covered with poison hemlock. In the middle of the island there is a large mound of stones, which appear to have been transported there in the past for a large building.

Before the island, at a short distance, one can see many houses scattered on the shore, which form the village of Canara (a Turkish word that means "rock").

D. Contogiorgi wrote that the village of Canara was on an island in the lagoon and that, according to the natives, it contains the house of an important person:

---

[242]Bruto Amante, Italian journalist and writer. Among other things, after a visit to Romania (Constanța) he published a work entitled *Ovid in Exile*.

On a land near the lagoons cattle graze, and this place is called Tomes, as was told by the Tartar primat[243] and hogi,[244] with whom I talked with the help of my dragoman,[245] Năstase al lui Ion Adrianopolitanului, who has lived in this village for a long time, trading in food products. My dragoman also told me that two large stones with Hellenic inscriptions had been transported with his own wagon, and that there were many other stones like those in the walls of the houses of the Tartar naigai,[246] in which no one could enter. Beyond the village of Canara, toward the northeast, there is a vast plain covered with remnants of columns, with carved stones and window frames ornated with flowers, remainders of large buildings. At the other extremity, toward the east, there is a sand isthmus that surrounds the lagoon.

Over time, the premise of Brute Amante became a working hypothesis to which the scholars of the Museum of National History and Archeology in Constanța gave course by initiating excavations based on the presence of certain surface clues.

In light of the discoveries made, we can draw the following conclusion: the island was inhabited for a long period of time during antiquity, both during the primitive commune period, as well as during the Greco-Roman era. This was natural, since the lake presented favorable conditions for the development of human life,

---

[243] *Primat* – the head of a village.

[244] Muslim priest.

[245] Here with the meaning of translator, Oriental interpreter.

[246] A Muslim minority, of Mongolian origin, whose name was taken from the first khan, Nogai. In the thirteenth century, they occupied a large region from Siberia to the Danube. Their central state was in the Crimea, where they were eventually conquered and dislocated by the Russians in 1783. Having retreated to Turkey, they live scattered in different regions, but many of them are still found today in the area of the north Caucasus Mountains.

including good conditions for agriculture and fishing. In addition, the island was easily defended by the waters of the lake.

During the Roman period, the island represented part of a vast settlement, situated on the other shore, in the southwest, where the latest archeological excavations have revealed a strong fortification.

This immediate vicinity and the similarity of the archeological materials found on the island with those discovered in the neighboring fortification – one of the numerous Roman camps – prove that the island was inhabited during Roman antiquity. Although the excavations did not uncover vestiges of Roman buildings, as archeologists had hoped they would, such structures did exist. This is evidenced by the numerous semi-chiseled stone blocks scattered on the shore of the island, as well as by the reports of the Italian traveler, Brute Amante.

Correlating the various elements of Roman material culture found on the island with the obscure legendary images, it is possible that this place of poetical inspiration, meditation, and spiritual recreation, was the refuge place of the author of *Tristia* and *Epistulae ex Ponto*. Perhaps it was in the village on the island or in a neighboring one, over which the Turkish village of Canara was later built, that Ovid became acquainted with the rough looking Getae, to whom he dedicated so many verses.

It is possible that, as a result of his repeated and long visits on the island and the neighboring *vicus*, the poet remained in the memory of the people who immortalized him in stories transmitted from generation to generation, until today. Moreover, tradition, related by Bruto Amante, says that the grave of Ovid is in a hidden place of the island. This information that comes from an uncertain source is not credible. More likely is the account provided in literary sources which state that the remains of the poet were buried in the city of Tomis, near the main gate of the defensive wall, which was standing at the beginning of the Christian era, when Roman power had just arrived at the Pontus Euxinus.

Most historians have agreed that Lake Ovid was a formal name, given to the lake by some English technicians who worked there between 1857 and 1860 on the railway linking Constanța and Cernavodă. The generalization of the name was the result of a topographical survey organized by Romanian officers after 1880 for the purpose of demonstrating the Roman-Dacian origin of the Romanian people.

Acta conventus omnium getium ovidianis studiis fovendis – Documents of the Congress on Ovidian Studies (Bucharest, 1976), includes an article entitled "Le lieu de la rélégation d'Ovide selon certains sources du Moyen âge" by Constantin C. Giurescu, in which he discussed a map made by the Viennese Tobias Conrad Lottar, entitled "Transylvania, Moldavia, Wallachia, and the New Bulgaria and their Delimitations." This cartographic document, dating from 1722, mentions, north of *Tomiswar,* a lake called *Ovidovo Iezero –* the above-mentioned Siutghiol. This information creates confusion. First of all, how did the geographer know at that time how to locate Tomiswar, Küstendje, when it is well-known that an exact, scientific determination was only made one hundred and fifty years later; secondly, because the lake is named after Ovid. If we accept that the city of Küstendje was identified with Tomis due to investigations that we are not aware of, in the case of the name of the lake, we believe that the explanation is a different source, probably some anonymous travelers to Dobrogea. Whatever the explanation may be, we have both a lake and an island, both of which have been named "Ovid" since the eighteenth century.

The ardent searches for Ovid's grave became more intense as time passed. After 1878, the attention of the entire public opinion of

Constanţa was concentrated on realizing this goal. Any important archeological discovery represented a possibility for uncovering a clue. But such a discovery in Constanţa became increasingly unlikely since the modernization and growth of the city made systematic investigations impossible within its precincts or in the necropolis. Nevertheless, opportunities presented themselves as a result of urban renewal efforts and new construction; often the resulting finds proved richer and more spectacular in their results than actual archeological excavations.

In 1931, when the sea wall in the southwestern part of the city of Constanţa was being stabilized, along the road that led "to the vineyards," a large marble sarcophagus was uncovered, whose refined execution and strange shape stirred the interest of the inhabitants of the city, as well as of the national and international press and scientific community.

Rigorous research undertaken and with great care and competence by Constantin Brătescu,[247] the director of the Regional Museum of Dobrogea, was often made difficult by the curiosity of the journalists as well as the insistence of the public who anxiously awaited the discovery of "Ovid's Sarcophagus." Irresponsible journalists began to proclaim the sarcophagus of the exiled poet had finally been discovered. The researchers were not distracted from their task by these unfounded assertions circulated by the journals of the time. Instead they patiently and tactfully went about their work to learn the truth about this discovery. According to Constantin

---

[247]Romanian geographer (1882-1945), professor at the University of Cernăuţi and then at the University of Bucharest. He was a corresponding member of the Romanian Academy. He made important contributions to the study of the Black Sea and Dobrogea, including *Oscilaţiile de nivel al apelor din bazinul Mării Negre, în cuaternar, Delta Dunării.* He directed the publication of *Analele Dobrogei* and was director of the Regional Museum of Dobrogea.

Brătescu: "From the first day of its discovery, only one name was on everyone's lips: "Ovid! Ovid's grave has been discovered!" From the public, the name was passed on by the press and reached as far as Sulmo and Paris."[248]

This precious relic, one of the most important pieces in the collection of the Museum of Constanța today, became the object of long and assiduous study, and numerous articles that have been written about it over the years, reaching different interpretations and conclusions. The symbols on the frontispiece surrounding the frame, in the shape of a *tabula ansata*,[249] on which there is no engraved epigraph, has been the subject of different interpretations and of much controversy. One hypothesis maintains that the person buried there was a merchant of animals. Another interpretation claims that the symbols represent the juridical attributes of a high magistrate or of a worshiper of the Oriental god Men.[250] It is only in recent years that it has been established with certainty that the sarcophagus dates from the second or third century A.D., being made of marble brought from Asia Minor, and that it belonged to a high magistrate – one of the *agoranoms* of Tomis, whose name was not mentioned in the epitaph.

The historic act of 9 May 1877, when Romania gained its freedom and independence, the natural consequence of this being the reintegration of Dobrogea within the borders of Romania, also

---

[248]Constantin Brătescu, "Sarcofagul cu simboluri din Constanța," in *Analele Dobrogei*, XII, 1931, p. 232.

[249]A rectangular frame, in the shape of a table, with the vertical margins uniting in the middle with the tips of isosceles triangles, looking like handles (in Latin, *ansa - ae*, hence the name mentioned above. Usually they were destined for the carving of funeral texts, as we see on sarcophaguses from the Roman period.

[250]*Dicționar de istorie veche...*, See "Culte orientale în Dacia și Scythia Minor."

marked a deeper penetration into the national consciousness of the fact, supported by overwhelming historical and archeological evidence, that the Romanian people form a large neo-Latin population at the Lower Danube. Everywhere in the Carpathians, on the plateaus of Moldavia, on the plains of Wallachia, and in the land of Dobrotici, testimonies of incontestable significance were gathered attesting to the Dacian-Roman origin of the Romanians. Trajan's Column in Rome, the Triumphal Monument at Adamclisi, Ovid in Constanţa, and the entire patrimony of material and spiritual culture discovered since 1878 formed the basis to legitimate the presence of the Romanian people within the boundaries established long ago by Burebista and Decebal.

This justifies the deference that the men of letters of the time granted to the great Latin poet. The bard from Mirceşti, Vasile Alecsandri,[251] realized, in inspired verses, the great bridge across two millennia on which Ovid's muse met with the muse of "the king of poetry," in a dialog perfectly knitted in the successful drama entitled *Ovidiu*, played on stage for the first time in 1885, in Bucharest.

It was in response to this awareness of their ethnic heritage that the people of Constanţa commissioned the statue of Ovid in the heart of the city. Its placement in the ancient agora served as an occasion that strengthened relations between Romania and Italy, and between Constanţa and Sulmo. The festivity of the unveiling of the statue was an opportunity for the celebration of the ethnic and linguistic consciousness of the Romanians. That occasion anticipated other

---

[251] A great Romanian poet and politician. As a politician, he participated in and led many important actions during the Revolution of 1848, and during the Union of the Romanian principalities in 1859. As a poet and playwright, he brought important contributions to Romanian culture: *Poezii populare ale românilor; Doine şi lăcrămioare; Legende; Ostaşii noştri; Pasteluri; Iorgu de la Sadaruga; Iaşii în carnival; Ciclul Chiriţelor* (the last three are comedies). Historical dramas: *Despot Vodă, Fântâna Blanduziei, Ovidiu,* etc.

Statue of Ovid
by the Italian sculptor Ettore Ferrari

special moments that took place later to strengthen ties between the city in which Ovid was born and the city in which the Getae comforted the suffering poet during his exile and at his death. The replica of the statue, erected in 1925 by the inhabitants of Sulmo, who raised in the poet's birthplace the same statue by Ettore Ferrari, using the original mold from 1883-1887, confirmed the spiritual connection between the two cities.

The common bond through Ovid is the basis for the act of sisterhood between Constanţa and Sulmo signed on 6 June 1968 in Constanţa, when the then mayors of the two cities, Petre Nicolae and Paolo di Bartolomeo, signed an accord recognizing that the great poet linked the two cities for eternity.

Acquitted by means of a trial that took place in Sulmo in 1967 from the unjust accusations brought upon him by blind imperial ambition, the gentle and innocent Ovid appears today before posterity as a majestic poetical personality, to whom we often dedicate the joy of meetings in the places where he was raised, created, and suffered. The Romanians and the Italians, with their thoughts, hearts, and actions raise the name of the poet to the highest peaks of the lyrical art and of humanism, whose universal messenger Ovid remains.

SELECTED BIBLIOGRAPHY

Acta conventus omnium gentium Ovidianis studiis fovendis. Bucureşti, 1976.

Amante, Bruto. *Ovidiu în exil.* Bucureşti, 1898 (trad. Cecilia Bruzzesi).

Aricescu, A. *Armata în Dobrogea romană.* Bucureşti: Editura Militară, 1977.

Atti del Convegno internazionale Ovidiano. Sulmo, 1959, Roma: Instituto di studi romani, 1959.

Barbu, Vasile. *Tomis, oraşul poetului exilat.* Bucureşti, 1972.

Barnea, I. and Ştefănescu, Şt. *Din istoria Dobrogei: Bizantini, români şi bulgari la Dunărea de Jos.* Bucureşti Academiei, 1971.

Benedum, Z. *Studien zur Dichtkunst des späten Ovids,* Giessen, 1967.

Bernbeck, E.Z. *Boebachtung zur Darstellung in Ovids Metamorphosen,* München, 1967.

Bernini, F. *Ovidio.* Tomis, 1938.

Bezdechi, St. "Ultimii ani ai lui Ovidiu la Tomis," in *Scrisori din Tomis,* Cluj, 1930, pp. III-XIV.

Bordenache, G. *Sculpture greche e romane nel Museo Nazionale do Antichita di Bucarest,* I. Bucureşti, 1969.

Bulgăr, Gh. "Ovidiu în peisajul dobrogean," in *Studii de literatura universală,* II. Bucureşti, 1960, pp. 69-77.

Bouynot. *La poésie d'Ovide dans les oeuvres de l'exil.* Paris, 1957.

Cahen, R. *Le rythme poétique dans les Métamorphoses d'Ovide*. Paris, 1910.

Castiglioni, S. *Studi intorno alle fonte e alla composizione delle Metamorfosi di Ovidio*, ed. II. Roma, 1964.

Comto, Fernand. *The Wordsworth Dictionary of Mythology*. Edinburgh: W&R Chambers, Ltd., 1991.

Danov, Chr. M. "Pontos Euxeinos," in *R.E. Supplld.*, IX, 1962, col. 866-1176.

De la Ville di Mirmont, H. *La jeunese d'Ovide*. Paris, 1905.

D'Elia, S. *Ovidio*. Napoli, 1959.

D'Elia, S. "L'esilio di Ovidio e alcuni aspetti della eta augustea", în *Annali Fac. Lettere dell'Univ. di Napoli*, 3. 1955, pp. 95-157.

Dessau, H. *Geschichte der römischen Kaiserzeit*, vol. I. Berlin, 1924; vol. II, 1928.

Dicţionar de istorie veche a României (Paleolitic – sec. X). Ed. D.M. Pippidi, Bucureşti: Editura Ştiinţifică şi Enciclopedică, 1976.

Drîmba, Ov. *Ovidiu, poetul Romei şi al Tomisului*, second edition. Bucureşti, 1966.

Favez, C. "Les G tes et leurs pays vus par Ovide," in *Latomus*. 1951, p. 425 ff.

Filow, B. *Die Legionen der Provinz Moesia von Augustus bis auf Diokletian*. Leipzig, 1906.

Fitz, J. *Die Laufbahn der Statthalter in der römischen Provinz Moesia Inferior*. Weimar: Herman Böhlaus, 1966.

Fränkel, H. *Ovid, a Poet between Two Worlds*. Berkeley-Los Angeles, 1945.

Frazer, J.G. *The Fasti of Ovid*. London, 1929.

Gandeva, B. "Moralische und soziale Charakteristik der West – and Nordbalkan bevölkerung bei Varro and Ovid," in *Actes du premier Congrés International des Études Balkaniques et Sud-Est Europeénnes*, II. Sofia, 1970, pp. 127-132.

Gerov, B. "L'aspect ethnique et linguistique dans la région entre le Danube et les Balkans," in *Studi Urbinati*. 1959, pp. 173-191.

Istoria României. Editura Academiei, 1960.

Izvoarele privind istoria României, I. Editura Academiei, Bucureşti, 1964.

Lascu, N. "Izvoarele literare ale Metamorforelor lui Ovidiu," in *Anuarul Inst. Stud. Clas.*, III. 1936-1938, pp. 74-137.

Lascu, N. "Notize di Ovidio sui Geto-Daci," in *Maia*. 1958, p. 307 ff.

Lascu, N. *Ovidiu, omul şi poetul*. Cluj, 1971.

Lamacchia, R. "Ovidio interprete di Virgilio," in *Maia*, 12. 1960, p. 310 ff.

Lavagnini, B. "La cronologia degli Amores," in *Atheneum*. 1921, p. 94 ff.

Lozovan, E. "Ovide, agonoth te de Tomis," in *Rel.*, XXXIX. 1961, pp. 172-181.

Ludwig, W. *Struktur and Einheit der Metamorphosen Ovids*. Berlin, 1965.

Mariotti, S. "La cariera poetica di Ovidio," in *Belfagor*, XII. 1957, pp. 609-635.

Marquardt, J. *Organisation de l'Empire Romain*. 2 vols., Paris, 1889.

Maşkin, N.A. *Principatul lui Augustus*. Moscova-Leningrad, 1949 (trad. rom. Bucureşti, 1954).

Maşkin, N.A. *Istoria Romei antice*. OGIZ, 1947.

Menzione, A. *Ovidio, Le Metamorfosi. Sintesi critice e contributo per una rivalutazione.* Torino, 1964.

Mic dicţionar al scriitorilor greci şi latini. Bucureşti: Editura Ştiinţifică şi Enciclopedică, 1978.

Miller, F.I. "Ovid's Aeneas and Vergil's: A Contrast in Motivation," in *Class Journ.*, 1927, p. 33 ff.

Mommsen, Th. *Römische Geschicte*, Wien-Leipzig: Phaidon Verlag, nd.

Nageotte, O. *Ovide, sa vie et ses oeuvres.* Dijon, 1872.

Noi monumente epigrafice din Schythia Minor. Constanţa, 1964.

Otis, B. *Ovid as an Empire Poet.* Cambridge, 1966, ed. II, 1970.

Ovid. *The Erotic Poems. Penguin Classics.* Translated by Peter Green. London: Penguin Books, 1982.

Ovid. *Fasti. Loeb Classical Library.* Translated by James G. Frazier, Revised by G.P. Goold. Cambridge, London: Harvard University Press, 1996.

Ovid. *Heroides/Amores. Loeb Classical Library.* Translated by Grant Showerman, Revised by G.P. Gould. Cambridge, London: Harvard University Press, 1996.

Ovid. *Metamorphoses.* Translated by Rolfe Humphries. Bloomington: Indiana University Press, 1983.

Ovid. *The Metamorphoses of Ovid.* Translated by Allen Mandelbaum. San Diego, New York, London: Harcourt, Brace & Company, 1993.

Ovid. *Tristia/Ex Ponto. Loeb Classical Library.* Translated by A.L. Wheeler, Revised by G.P. Gould. Cambridge, London: Harvard University Press, 1996.

Ovidiu. *Metamorfoza.* Editura Academiei, Bucureşti, 1959.

Ovidiu. *Fastele*. Editura Academiei, Bucureşti, 1965.

Ovidiu. *Tristele*, Ponticele. Bucureşti, 1972.

Ovidiu. *Arta iubirii*. Bucureşti, 1977.

Ovidiana. *Recherches sur Ovide, publiées á l'occasion du bimillénnaire de la naissance du poéte*. Paris, 1958.

Paratore, E. *Motivi umami nella poesia di Ovidio*. Sulmona, 1956.

Paratore, E. *Bibliographia Ovidiana*. Sulmona, 1958.

Pârvan, V. *Începuturile vieţii romane la gurile Dunării*. Bucureşti, 1923.

Pârvan, V. *Zidul cetăţii Tomis*. Bucureşti, 1915 (ARMSI, ser. II, t. XXX-VII).

Pfeiffer, Z. *Untersuchungen zur Komposition und Erzähltechnik von Ovids Fasten*. Tübingen, 1952.

Pichon, R. *Histoire de la littérature latine*. Paris, 1898.

Pick, B. *Die antiken Müzen von Dacien and Moesien*, I. Berlin, 1898.

Pippidi, D.M. *Scythia Minora. Recherches sur les colonies greques du littoral roumain de la Mer Noir*. Bucureşti: Editura Academiei; Amsterdam: Adolf M. Hakkert B.V., 1975.

Pippidi, D.M. and Berciu D. *Din istoria Dobrogei: Geţi şi greci la Dunărea de Jos*. Bucureşti: Editura Academiei, 1965.

Pontica I-XXIX. Muzeul de arheologie Constanţa, 1968-1996.

Premerstein A. von. *Die Anfänge der Provinz Moesien*, JÖAI, I. 1898, Beibl., cols. 145-196.

Publius Ovidius Naso. vol. colectiv, Bucureşti: Editura Academiei, 1957.

Rădulescu, A. and Bitoleanu, I. *Istoria Dobrogei*, 1979.

Regling, K. *Die antiken Münzen von Dacien and Moesien*, II. Berlin, 1910.

Ripert, E. *Ovide poète l'amour, des dieux et de l'èxil*. Paris, 1921.

Romano, V. *Geneologiae deorum gentilium*, II. Bari, 1901.

Rostovzef, M. *Storia economica e sociale delle'Impero Romano*. Firenze, 1953.

Salvatore, A. *Aspetti della sensibilita e delle'arte di Ovidio*. Napoli, 1966.

Schilling, R. "Ovide, po te sed Fastes," in *Mélanges Carcopino*. Paris, 1966, p. 863 ff.

Schilling, R. "Ovide, interpréte de la religion romaine," in *Et. Lat.*, XLVI. 1968, p. 222 ff.

Stein, A. *Die Legaten von Moesien*. Budapest, 1940.

Stoian, I. *Tomitana, Contribuții epigrafice la istoria cetății Tomis*. București, 1962.

Storia della letteratura latina, I. Bologna, 1969.

Studi Ovidiani a cura dell'Istituto di Studi Romani. Roma, 1959.

Suceveanu, Al. *Viața economică în Dobrogea romană sec I-III e.n.* București: Editura Academiei, 1977.

Teodorescu, D.M. *Monumente inedite din Tomis*. București, 1918.

Tezaurul de sculpturi de la Tomis. Editura Științifică, 1963.

Thibalt, J.C. *The Mystery of Ovid's Exile*. Berkeley-Los Angeles, 1964.

Tissier, A. *La société romaine dans l'oeuvre d'Ovide*. Paris, 1944.

Tocilescu, Gr. *Fouilles et recherches archéologiques en Roumanie*, București, 1900.

Toutain, J. "La religion romaine d'après les Fastes d'Ovide," in *Journal des savants*, 1931, p. 105 ff.

Tremoli, P. *Infussi retorici e inspirazione poetica negli Amores di Ovidio.* Trieste, 1955.

Trozzi, M. *Ovidio e i suoi tempi.* Catania, 1930.

Viarre, S. *L'image at la pensée dans les Métamorphoses d'Ovide.* Paris, 1964.

Viarre, S. Ovide, *Essai de lectures poétique.* Paris, 1976.

Vigevani, A. "Stile ed imitazione nelle Metamorfosi do Ovidio," in *Atti Academia Scienze,* Lettere ed Arti di Udine, 1960.

Vulpe, Radu and Barnea, Ion. *Din istoria Dobrogei: Romanii la Dunărea de Jos.* Bucureşti: Editura Academiei, 1968.

Vulpe, R. *Histoire ancienne de la Dobroudja.* Bucureşti, 1938.

Wagner, W. *Die Dislokation der römischen Auxiliarformationen in den Provinzen Noricum, Pannonien, Moesien and Dakien von Augustus bis Gallienus.* Berlin, 1938.

Weiss, J. *Die Dobrudscha* im Alertum. Sarajevo, 1911.

Wilkinson, L.P. *Ovid Recalled.* Cambridge, 1955.

Wilkinson, L.P. *Ovid Surveyed. An Abridgement for the General Reader of "Ovid Recalled."* Cambridge, 1962.

INDEX

HISTRIA BOOKS

ALSO AVAILABLE:

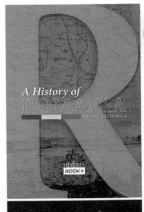

HISTRIA

HISTRIABOOKS.COM